Globalization Alternatives

Globalization Alternatives

Strategies for the
New International Economy

J. Mark Munoz

BEP BUSINESS EXPERT PRESS

Globalization Alternatives: Strategies for the New International Economy
Copyright © Business Expert Press, LLC, 2018.

First published in 2018 by
Business Expert Press, LLC
222 East 46th Street, New York, NY 10017
www.businessexpertpress.com

ISBN-13: 978-1-63157-778-9 (paperback)
ISBN-13: 978-1-63157-779-6 (e-book)

Business Expert Press International Business Collection

Collection ISSN: 1948-2752 (print)
Collection ISSN: 1948-2760 (electronic)

Cover and interior design by S4Carlisle Publishing Services Private Ltd., Chennai, India

First edition: 2018

10 9 8 7 6 5 4 3 2 1

Printed in the United States of America.

Abstract

In a complex and growingly chaotic global environment, individuals, companies, and countries are forced to adapt, innovate, and operate in new ways. Creative and unconventional economic and business models are constantly being developed in order for countries and corporations to gain a competitive advantage. Countless novel ideas have challenged traditional views on the merits of globalization.

Populist and protectionist sentiments have gained ground alongside calls for economic nationalism, alter-globalization, deglobalization and even unglobalization. Skepticism is on the rise, and there is a pressing need for fresh solutions and viable strategies. This book assembled a cast of international experts and thought leaders and gathered their views on alternative pathways toward global success.

Keywords

Alter-global, deglobalization, economic nationalism, global strategy, globalization, globalization alternative, international strategy, unglobalization

Contents

SECTION 1

Introduction

CHAPTER 1

Introduction

J. Mark Munoz

Globalization refers to social, economic, political, and cultural inter-connectedness across countries (Ohmae 1995). It is both a fact and phenomena and foundation for many events around the world.

For many countries, it is the cornerstone for growth and development. Economic and trade liberalization is an important foundation for GDP growth (Soubbotina 2004; Giavazzi and Tabellini 2005). Financial and product market openness attracts capital, resources, and talent among others (Mishkin 2009). Globalization impacts macroeconomic factors such as inflation, output, and interest rates (Milani 2012). Evidences suggest that trade and financial openness impacts financial development (Baltagi et al. 2009; Kim et al. 2010).

Globalization runs deep into the core of contemporary business, economics, and politics. With its impact on reducing inequality and minimizing corruption, globalization creates a more democratic environment (Acemoglu and Robinson 2005). Mishkin (2009) indicated that economic globalization leads to institutional reforms and enhances its quality. Stultz (1999) indicated that globalization forces governments to improve legal and infrastructure systems.

The nature and architecture of globalization makes it a dynamo for change. Recent global events have shown a paradigm shift in traditional notions of politics, business, and economics. As examples, UK's Brexit vote and USA's 2016 Presidential election, which brought billionaire businessman Donald Trump to power, suggest that there has been heightened interest in experimentation and the pursuit of the unconventional.

In many corners of the world, political leaders have taken on populist and even protectionist standpoints. Policy makers have started to take a close look at programs promoting economic nationalism. Entrepreneurs have planned and implemented innovative models that defy conventional wisdom. Economists have started to explore radical concepts and theories.

Meanwhile, amidst this fast-changing and evolving global business environment, many have started to question the merits of globalization. Several tough questions have emerged: Does globalization benefit all countries and citizens around the world? Do some reap its rewards more than others? Is globalization for the privileged few? Are the billions of poorly educated and poverty stricken detached from the globalization loop? Are there adverse social, cultural, environmental, and financial consequences to globalization? Should new globalization models be explored? Should countries and firms be "unglobal" and detach itself from the rest of the world? How should countries, companies, and individuals manage the strong and ever-changing forces of globalization?

Critics claim that globalization has led to intense competition for the lowest costs and most appealing economic policies (Stiglitz 2002; Milanovic 2003). It puts a pressure on policy challenges that impact emerging economies (Law et al. 2014). It has adverse effect on public spending (Busemeyer 2009).

Others claim that low-cost producing countries in a global environment place pressure on wages and prices of goods in the industrialized countries (Borio and Filardo 2007; Pehnelt 2010). It has created an environment of consumer ethnocentrism and economic nationalism (Shimp and Sharma 1987; Baughn and Yaprak 1996). Financial and trade liberalization has created macroeconomic volatility leading to financial crises (Eatwell and Taylor 2000). There are challenges in accounting and the treatment of financial statements to deal with (Bryan et al. 2010).

Globalization touches many levels in a society. It has negative social and environmental effects (Harris and Nef 2008). It creates hybridization of cultures and economic structures (Nederveen Pieterse 2004). Furthermore, there is cause for concern for human and social rights (Baccaro 2010; Hafner-Burton 2005).

While there are criticisms about globalization, there are also many praises. For instance, there are economic benefits from globalization as a result of investments, trade, technology gains, and job creation (Kucera 2002; Flanagan 2006). Trade openness can contribute to financial development (Svaleryd and Vlachos 2002). Globalization of banking has led to several benefits (Goldberg 2009).

There is heightened sense of global connectedness among people (Strizhakova and Coulter 2015). A sense of global identity and world-mindedness has been created (Bartikowski and Walsh 2015; Nijssen and Douglas 2008). There has been a notable mobility of labor (Grogger and Hanson 2011). There has been observed homogenization and standardization (Ritzer 1993).

It can enhance governance in some nations. Trade openness decreases corruption (Ades and Di Tella 1999). Trade and financial openness will lead to wage increases and reduce inequality (Acemoglu and Robinson 2005). Emerging nations with open economies have significantly improved their world trade networks (International Monetary Fund 2006).

In the case of business, corporate overseas operations tend to complement domestic operations (Hayakawa et al. 2013). Many businesses have successfully expanded operations overseas and sold their products worldwide.

Debates continue worldwide on the actual merits and demerits of globalization. Conversations would likely linger for years due to many unanswered questions and unresolved issues.

This book would not be able to tackle all key issues regarding contemporary globalization. Instead, it aims to offer selected fresh perspectives on the subject of globalization alternatives from innovative thinkers from around the world. The intent is not to offer an all-encompassing and universal approach to alter globalization. Instead, the book's goal is to focus on a few key issues to help the reader deliberate and assess potential merits of the selected globalization ideas. After this assessment, the reader can utilize certain aspects of the idea to develop a customized personal or organizational plan for success. In the concluding chapter of this book, suggestions and guidelines are offered for the strategic management of globalization.

In an effort to enhance appreciation and understanding of contemporary globalization, its defining attributes are described below.

1. **Discontentment** – A multitude of individuals are unhappy or discontented with globalization. As a result of open border country policies, international trade and investment incentives, and heightened trade integration, some industries lost their competitive advantages and consequently experienced financial losses. Under this scenario, job losses were experienced in certain sectors. The fact that some countries offer subsidies and grants to certain industries lead to advantages that are deemed unfair by competitors who are not recipients of similar benefits.

2. **Diversity in approaches** – Countries manage globalization in different ways. Some countries create policies that embrace internationalization and free trade, and some prefer to take on more protectionist measures. A similar variation in approaches is noticeable among companies. There are companies that execute an aggressive internationalization strategy, whereas others focus solely on domestic markets.

3. **Geopolitical influences** – The confluence of geography, politics, and economics influence global events, trade, and relationships across nations. Countries that are geopolitically aligned may choose to limit trade dealings with those in opposing camps.

4. **Geoeconomic influences** – The economic relationships of countries consequently impact trade and political relations. For example, some sectors feel that the EU operates like a trade fortress where members prefer to collaborate with fellow members.

5. **Global versus local pressures** – Countries and companies feel both global and local pressures. Countries have to weigh in on the merits of enhancing global trade versus protecting local industries. When companies expand overseas, they need to consider the extent in which they pursue a one standard global strategy as opposed to responding to local preferences in each country.

6. **Uneven benefits across countries** – Countries around the world experience profit and loss in varying degrees as a result of globalization. For example, some countries benefit with attracting investment and expanding trade, whereas others suffer from capital flight and brain drain.

7. **Uneven benefits across industries** – Industries also experience profit and loss from globalization. Firms profit when investments pour in or when products find international markets, whereas firms lose when international competitors gain a foothold in their local market or when their top talent migrate to other countries for higher paying jobs.

8. **Accelerated by web and digital media platforms** – The internet and digital media platforms sped up and added convenience to cross-border communication. Gathering of information and business intelligence has improved rapidly in recent years.

9. **Influenced by cultural changes** – Globalization has also affected cultural transformation around the world. With facilitated international travel, cross-border business, and social media usage, consumer knowledge, sophistication, and tastes have evolved. For instance, in key cities in China the growing presence of French bakeshops are noticeable, along with high-end retail shops.

10. **Driven by advances in travel, tourism, transport, and logistics** – The travel, transport, and tourism industries have facilitated the movement of people and goods around the world. In both cases, the volume has been consistently growing. This scenario has led to the acceleration of globalization.

11. **Language and convenience** – Language has become less of a barrier to globalization and business. Bilinguals and multilinguals have been on the rise. Some languages have even started to evolve with the integration of foreign words in the vocabulary. Web and mobile apps with language translation features has facilitated cross-border global communication.

12. **Geographic cross-pollination** – There has also been heightened global mobility. Employees have been more open to overseas postings. Inter-racial marriages are becoming more common. Many individuals choose to retire in exotic international locales.

These are just some of the changes that define globalization. In greater likelihood, more changes will follow and a hyper-globalized world will be the norm.

This book hopes to uncover these emerging changes and its implications. The goal is to showcase new ideas, solutions, challenges, as well as complexities brought about by globalization.

The book is organized in five sections. Section 1 is Introduction (J. Mark Munoz). Section 2 covers Countries and Governance and includes "Globalization's Opposite: The Case of Bhutan" (Shelly Daly), "Strategic Globalization Alternative: The Case of Kenya" (Abel Kinoti Meru and Mary Wanjiru Kinoti), and "The Alternative of Pursuing Localization before Globalization: The Case of the City of Ferguson and International Media" (Shelly Daly). Section 3 pertains to Institutions and Policies and discusses "International Financial Institutions (IFIs): Facilitators or Obstructionists to Globalization? (Diana Heeb Bivona), Coping with State-Led Unglobalization: A Historical Analysis of Iran's Petroleum Industry (Alireza Saify, Joobin Ordoobody, and Jasper Hotho), and "Local Content Policies: Global versus National?" (Irina Heim). Section 4 showcases Businesses and Industries and expounds on "Unglobal Finance: Informal and Alternative Banking Activities" (Les Dlabay), "Birth and Growth in Isolation: Development of the Generic Pharmaceutical Industry in Bangladesh" (Md. Noor Un Nabi and Utz Dornberger), and "Buy Local: A Consumer's Alternative to the Global Market?" (Shelly Daly). Section 5 is the Conclusion (J. Mark Munoz).

Diverse sectors would benefit from this book. The academe would find fresh concepts to contemplate and debate on. Governments would find some of the ideas insightful in terms of policy formation. Businesses would find some of the information and mindsets useful in crafting internationalization strategies. Consulting companies, research firms, and international organizations would find the viewpoints useful in understanding the nuances of the new global environment. Finally, executives and entrepreneurs worldwide would find value on several innovative notions for global success.

This book is not meant to be a comprehensive volume that answers all questions and challenges brought about by globalization. It is, however, an important step toward expanding conversations and exploring innovative ideas for the enhancement of future global pathways.

References

Acemoglu, D., and J.A. Robinson. 2005. *Economic Origins of Dictatorship and Democracy*. Cambridge: Cambridge University Press.

Ades, A., and R. Di Tella. 1999. "Rents, Competition and Corruption", *The American Economic Review* 89, no. 4, pp. 982–993.

Baccaro, L. 2010. "Does the global financial crisis mark a turning point for labour?", *Socio-Economic Review* 8, no. 2, pp. 341–376.

Baltagi, B.H., P. Demetriades, and S.H. Law. 2009. "Financial Development and Openness: Panel Data Evidence", *Journal of Development Economics* 89, no. 2, pp. 285–296.

Bartikowski, B., and G. Walsh. 2015. "Attitude Toward Cultural Diversity: A Test of Identity-Related Antecedents and Purchasing Consequences", *Journal of Business Research* 68, no. 3, pp. 526–533.

Baughn, C., and A. Yaprak. 1996. "Economic Nationalism: Conceptual and Empirical Development", *Political Psychology* 17, no. 4, pp. 759–778.

Borio, C., and A. Filardo. 2007. "Globalization and Inflation: New Cross-country Evidence on the Global Determinants of Domestic inflation", BIS Working Paper, no. 227. Basel : Bank for International Settlements.

Bryan, S., S.B. Lilien, and Sarath, B. 2010. "Countering Opportunism in Structuring and Valuing Transactions: The Case of Securitizations", *Journal of Accounting, Auditing & Finance* 25, pp. 289–321.

Busemeyer, M. 2009. "From Myth to Reality: Globalisation and Public Spending in OECD Countries Revisited", *European Journal of Political Research* 48, no. 4, pp. 455–482.

Eatwell, J., and L. Taylor. 2000. *Global Finance at Risk*. New York: The New Press.

Flanagan, R. 2006. *Globalization and Labor Conditions: Working Conditions and Worker Rights in a Global Economy*. New York: Oxford University Press.

Giavazzi, F., and G. Tabellini. 2005. "Economic and Political Liberalizations", *Journal of Monetary Economics* 52, no. 7, pp. 1297–1330.

Goldberg, L. 2009. "Understanding Banking Sector Globalization", *International Monetary Fund Staff Papers* 56, pp. 171–197.

Grogger, J., and G.H. Hanson. 2011. "Income Maximization and the Selection and Sorting of International Migrants", *Journal of Development Economics* 95, no. 1, pp. 42–57.

Hafner-Burton, E.M. 2005. "Right or robust? The Sensitive Nature of Repression to Globalization", *Journal of Peace Research* 42, no. 6, pp. 679–698.

Harris, R.L., and J. Nef (eds.). 2008. *Capital, Power, and Inequality in Latin America and the Caribbean*. Lanham : Rowman & Littlefield Publishers, Inc.

Hayakawa, K., T. Matsuura, K. Motohashi, and A. Obashi. 2013. "Two-Dimensional Analysis of the Impact of Outward FDI on Performance at Home: Evidence from Japanese manufacturing firms", *Japan and the World Economy* 27, pp. 25–33.

International Monetary Fund (IMF). 2006. How Has Globalization Affected Inflation? Chapter III. In *IMF World Economic Outlook*. Washington, DC: USA/International Monetary Fund.

Kim, D., S. Lin, and Y. Suen. 2010. "Dynamic Effects of Trade Openness on Financial Development", *Economic Modelling* 27, no. 1, pp. 254–261.

Kucera, D. 2002. "Core Labour Standards and Foreign Direct Investment", *International Labour Review* 141, no. 1–2, pp. 31–69.

Law, S., W. Azman-Saini, and H. Tan. 2014. "Economic Globalization and Financial Development in East Asia: A panel Cointegration and Causality Analysis", *Emerging Markets Finance and Trade* 50, no. 1, pp. 210–225.

Milani, F. 2012. "Has Globalization Transformed U.S. Macroeconomic Dynamics?", *Macroeconomic Dynamics* 16, pp. 204–229.

Milanovic, B. 2003. "The Two Faces of Globalization: Against Globalization as We Know It", *World Development* 31, no. 4, pp. 667–683.

Mishkin, F.S. 2009. "Globalization and Financial Development", *Journal of Development Economics* 89, no. 2, pp. 164–169.

Nederveen Pieterse, J. 2004. *Globalization and Culture*. Lanham : Rowman and Littlefield, p. 160.

Nijssen, E.J., and S.P. Douglas. 2008. "Consumer World-Mindedness, Social-Mindedness, and Store Image", *Journal of International Marketing* 16, no. 3, pp. 84–107.

Ohmae, K. 1995. *The End of the Nation State*. New York: Free Press, p. 214.

Pehnelt, G. 2010. Globalisation and inflation in OECD countries. ECIPE Working Paper, no. 2007–2055. Brussels, Belgium: European Center for International Political Economy.

Ritzer, G. 1993. *The McDonaldization of Society*. London: Sage, p. 265.

Shimp, T.A., and S. Sharma.1987. "Consumer Ethnocentrism: Construction and Validation of the CETSCALE", *Journal of Marketing Research* 24, pp. 280–289.

Soubbotina, T. 2004. *Globalization: International Trade and Migration*. Washington, DC: World Bank.

Stiglitz, J.E. 2002. *Globalization and Its Discontents*. London: W. W. Norton.

Strizhakova, Y., and R.A. Coulter. 2015. "Drivers of Local Relative to Global Brand Purchases: A Contingency Approach", *Journal of International Marketing* 23, no. 1, pp. 1–22.

Stultz, R. 1999. "Globalization, Corporate Finance and the Cost of Capital", *Journal of Applied Corporate Finance* 12, no. 3, pp. 8–25.

Svaleryd, H., and J. Vlachos. 2002. "Markets for Risk and Openness to Trade: How Are They Related?", *Journal of International Economics* 57, no. 2, pp. 369–395.

SECTION 2

Countries and Governance

CHAPTER 2

Globalization's Opposite

The Case of Bhutan

Shelly Daly

The old model is broken. We need to create a new one. . . . we must unite around a shared vision for the future—a vision for equitable human development, a healthy planet, an enduring economic dynamism. Ban Ki-moon, the Secretary General of the United Nations

—As quoted by Alkire (2015)

Introduction

Imagine for a moment, a land that is far-far-away. Beautiful and majestic, peaceful and quiet. A land unto itself, a country with formidable borders that can easily keep others out and harmony in. Borders that are not armed or controlled, but rather peaceful dividing lines of demarcation for all they hold dear. Imagine this country has never been conquered or colonized, and its inhabitants live peacefully with nature, neighboring countries, and each other. Its rivers are pristine and blue-green, usually found in oceans, and are stocked full of fish since those who dwell in the land refuse to kill any other living thing. The food is organic, harvested, and shared. The kingdom loves its rulers with a devotion usually reserved for parents and children. People smile graciously and welcome you to their paradise with unparalleled hospitality and yet remain unsoiled by the cycles of marketing and capitalistic forces. Citizens of this tranquil land are free to come and go, and yet 95 percent of those who leave, return with enthusiasm and happiness.

As people imagined such a land, they sometimes used words like Shangri-La, or utopia, or paradise. Others thought of Disney stories and old fairy tales. However, these images do not compare to what really exists. This place is accessible, real, and preserved as few places can be in the 21st century.

This place of peace, beauty, and happiness is the Kingdom of Bhutan. A country nestled in the Himalayan mountains, between the international giants India and China. The view of Bhutan is one of success and isolation, advancement and tradition, and happiness and liberalization. As a nation, Bhutan has never been conquered or colonized, and their economy is based on Gross National Happiness (GNH), instead of gross domestic product (GDP) or gross national product (GNP). As a Democratic Monarchy since 2008, they have rejected traditional tenets of success and voted down the idea of joining the World Trade Organization (WTO) and United Nations (UN), while still increasing literacy rates, improving life expectancy and health standards, and developing a world-class education system. This country gives us a looking-glass to delve into understanding how every level of society functions against the backdrop of choosing something other than globalization.

Background

The population of Bhutan is around 750,000, with two-thirds of that number being rural inhabitants. It is roughly the size of Tennessee with 70 percent of the land heavily forested, and, until very recently, it was solely a farming-based economy. The monarchy has been in place for over 100 years and the kings and queens are beloved and revered. Democracy joined the government establishment in 2008 at the persistent urging and campaigning of its Fourth King. After becoming a democratic monarchy and elected parliament, the Fourth King abdicated and his internationally educated son began his rule. The World Bank states that the Bhutanese Gross National Income in 2014 was $2,409, up from $730 in 2000, which is one of the highest levels in South Asia. Likewise, its poverty rate is one of the lowest in South Asia at 2.2 percent.

A strong friendship and alliance with India has allowed Bhutan to develop road networks that, while still uneven, allow for cross-country transfer of goods and services. The average speed on the curvy, landslide-prone roads is about 25 mph. Ties with India also allowed for the growth of the hydropower sector and the economy. India also provides the base for military training, engineering, land planning, and construction services.

Development came swiftly to this Himalayan Kingdom with road projects and tourism beginning in the 1960s. Bhutan is currently in its 11th, 5-year plan, and green development and self-reliance are its hallmarks. The focus on GNH was first articulated by the Fourth King, but his son, the now reigning Fifth King, states that GNH is about "Development with Values." Bhutan is a country unique unto itself in many ways, but especially noteworthy for the value and equality it offers to its women. Women are afforded every right, equality, income, and social standing as men. Bias and discrimination seem nonexistent, and access to the upper levels of leadership and opportunity are readily evident for all citizens.

Government Focus

The Legal Code of Bhutan from 1729 states that "If the government cannot create happiness for its people, then there is no purpose for government to exist." According to the Provisional Findings of the 2015 GNH Survey, the development of the country cannot and should not occur unless material and spiritual development occur side-by-side. This thought and statement, more than any other, signifies the willingness of this tiny democratic monarchy to eschew the lure and pull of globalization on any terms except its very own. Happiness is closely linked with the lack of consumption. One day or even 1 hour in Bhutan will convince the most skeptical critic that the citizens are not only happy, but happy beyond any comparison that most Western thinkers can make.

To continue with the code of 1729, it then goes into other means of fostering happiness, such as the need to curb the consumption of resources by officials of the state. This is not an insignificant point because an overwhelming portion of revenue of the government can be consumed by the bureaucracy and state enterprises, allegedly to provide goods and services for the people, or gets inefficiently used. In modern jargon, we call such expenditure budget. . . education to create enlightened individuals has been a leading concern for most of the history in the Himalayas. This concern now knocks against education to develop civics and market competencies so that one becomes a good citizen in a narrow sense and has the requisite skills to find jobs in highly unstable economies. Economies are unstable because the markets, both abroad and domestic, expand and contract. (Provisional Findings of 2015 GNH Survey, p. 19)

In the 1970s, Bhutan's Fourth King was noted to repeatedly refer to the idea of happiness associated with development, and then later coined the term GNH. His speeches noted that while many nations modernized quite successfully, and the term was used consequently called modernization development, this conventional path to development overlooked a universal and pervasive desire for humans to be happy and at peace.

The entry of expatriates, UN membership, and bilateral agreements led to a number of ideas, suggestions, and reports on how to modernize Bhutan, but most failed to recognize the inherent value system within the country. Its citizens were left with no way to integrate the new ideas with their traditional life style. However, the formalization of a policy for GNH brought in this synergy and cohesion, and eventually led to the measures of modernization now seen in the country. This was not just new vocabulary, but new ideas, attitudes, and approaches employed to responding to the pull of globalization.

His Majesty's views may seem perfectly reasonable when viewed from the lens of two decades into the 21st century, when corporations embrace green technology and social responsibility. But for the 1970s, it was unparalleled and revolutionary in the circles of thinking and development of international business.

Now, more discussions are concerned with the quality of life, development centered on social consciousness, and a willingness to accept the satisfactions that come with a slower paced life, not necessarily replete with material wealth. In 2012, the UN named March 20 the "International Day of Happiness" as a reflection of a change in values and sentiments throughout the world. Bhutan laid the framework to understand this alternative to globalization by blending personal and economic development with a pursuit of something other than financial gain or well-being.

However, it is the need to blend government policy with personal fulfillment that makes GNH inherently difficult to adopt. Policy makers rarely make the effort or find the latitude needed to adhere to principles that its citizens are not even aware they lack. The GNH is communicated and articulated into broad policy directions which overarch the 5-year plans of the Bhutanese government and its long-term strategies. The four pillars of GNH philosophy are: sustainable development, preservation and promotion of cultural values, conservation of the natural environment, and establishment of good governance.

Thus, Bhutan's government must manage macroeconomic pressure on demand. The idea of personal credit was only introduced a few years ago and is still not widely accepted or used. Very few citizens carry any form of credit card and even fewer succumb to the lure of purchasing on credit at stores that offer in-house plans. The country's constitution requires that 60 percent of the country must remain forested and the current percentage hovers in the high 70s. Pictures of the royal family and lineage dominate every business, home, and public space and there is a genuine love for and admiration for heritage represented in the monarchy. While the pillars of GNH seem firmly embedded, their foundation could be easily dismantled by forces of a demand-driven economy.

The monarchy and government leaders support and promote entrepreneurship and development. However, the population seems flummoxed at times on how to balance development and GNH. The current response to blending the two seems to be an inward focus with new business start-ups offering existing products and services internally, in a new area or region of the county. Such a model of development is not sustainable, and while the government may be aware of this, it seems a harder task to communicate it to the general population. The obvious answer would appear to be development of a larger export market centered on Bhutanese cultural products, agriculture, and natural resources, centered on small- and medium-sized enterprises .

Local government leaders throughout the districts comprising the small country have been provided a GNH checklist to guide village leaders toward development that fits with national government pillars of happiness and the constitutional framework. The private business sector will eventually be the driving force for the direction of the country, and the government seems to be paving the way to continue the solid ground of development that has occurred over the last 50 years, which has allowed Bhutan to remain independent, internally goal-oriented, and pursuant of a framework that is unique and unlike the traditional models of globalization.

Bhutan's Example

Globalization is achieved when historically distinct and independent markets merge. National boundaries often become blurred in a market-place where Internet-driven sales and global supply chains and distribution channels abound, and cross-border sourcing and price comparisons are the norm. In accepted views and definitions of globalization, national economies are interdependent, consumer preferences converge, and perceived distance is shrinking. Under any of these parameters, it is easy to see that while Bhutan is a global player, they have chosen a path that is not based on the forces, mechanisms, or lure of globalization.

Nine distinct domains support the measurement of the four pillars of GNH. They are:

Psychological well-being
Community vitality
Time use and balance
Cultural diversity and resilience
Health
Education
Good governance
Ecological diversity and resilience
Living standard

The government of Bhutan views the first four pillars on this list to be independent of material consumption and income. The nine domains are viewed as interdependent and nonlinear in nature and none seem to be viewed as more important or significant than the other. A detailed, meticulous, and professional survey of the 20 dzongkhags (districts) is taken every 5 years to measure and ascertain levels of happiness based on the four pillars and nine domains. For GNH, economic growth is not an end in itself, but a means for holistic development, given that it balances economic needs with emotional, spiritual, cultural, ecological, political, and social needs (Verma and Ura 2015).

The government currently supports an army of 6,000, the only military branch present in the Kingdom. Additionally, it supports a network of over 20,000 monks throughout the country. There are no indications of a change in this ratio or focus on government expenditures in these areas. However, the comparative ratio of these two numbers is part of the discussion and interest in understanding the unique composition and focus on globalization's alternative for this country.

Another interesting number in understanding the choices and progression of the Bhutanese economic system is the farming sector. In the recent past, their economy was based almost exclusively on agriculture. Even as recently as the year 2000, 80 percent of the economy was farming based, and in 2016, it was 56 percent. To make such remarkable strides to change the economic composition by half within 30 years, with no dramatic change in political leadership, war, or other causal event, is remarkable. To do so and still remain primarily self-reliant and with minimal emphasis on consumption or lifestyle changes is even more noteworthy. Bhutan remains committed to the alternative viewpoint and approach to globalization and the example it has set for most every other nation.

Ura et al. (2015) state, "At a moment when market-oriented, techno-centric and consumption-led approaches prevail in response to otherwise complex sociocultural and political-economic realities, innovative concepts from Bhutan present an alternative bearing on equitable, sustainable, and holistic development." In July of 2011, Bhutan adopted Resolution 65/309 titled *Happiness: Towards a holistic approach to development* and hosted a 2012 UN meeting on the topic in New York. According to the New Development Paradigm (NDP) report (2013), "The time has never been more opportune to re-orient the goal of development toward genuine human happiness and the well-being of all life."

Conclusion

The NDP states more specifically and certainly than other written documentation toward understanding and accepting that the Himalayan Kingdom of Bhutan has chosen an alternative path to globalization. While pursuing an economy that can flourish, they have chosen a unique approach that requires systematic and thoughtful decision making, which can transform the citizen's relationship to wealth, while restricting the economy. It will require unorthodox and untested methods, careful exploration, and conscious decision making to keep man and nature in harmony.

Current paths to globalization embrace ideas of limitless growth and infinite wants while surreptitiously depleting limited natural resources. A new path, an alternative to globalization as traditionally known, seems to make intuitive sense when viewed through the lens of interrelatedness of humans, earth, and plant and animal species that the Bhutanese have built their development on. Development is a necessity. All countries, human beings, and nations would undeniably accept that development can, must, and should continue. One country has offered a path that is unlike that of the means and objectives pursued under traditional models of international business.

The leaders and people of Bhutan have pursued their alternative path of development in a way and means that is prudent and successful for their country. However, there are aspects of this path that are particularly of interest to Western nations for replicability. The success of Bhutan comes alongside a country fighting an uphill battle to preserve its culture and way of life. If they can successfully seek, find, and implement an alternative path of development, it stands to reason that other countries could too. For example, the move to organic farming and green and sustainable measures for all industry. Their use of specific trade agreements with neighboring India in order to increase regional cooperation and development is also a model for Western governments pursuing alternatives to rampant and uncontrolled development.

This being said, the macroeconomic policies that control pressures on consumer demand and credit may not be easily implemented in highly developed countries that currently sustain growth via pressure on credit supply. Additionally, enforcing sustainable development laws for newer industries will come with the pressure of comparison on benefits of previous, noncompliant development.

The use of traditional measures of growth and economic development failed to account for unpaid work, well-being or declines in living standards. By studying and understanding an alternative path to the global marketplace, progress can also be made by displacing the limitations of previous measures of economic development. A close look at choices made by the leaders of Bhutan can offer innumerable lessons to global leaders. For example, the well-being of Bhutanese citizens being enhanced by choices to limit import of eggs and chicken allowed farmers to continue with gainful employment and in-country distribution of these products. The elimination of public smoking as a country-wide policy has positively impacted health, while decreasing the outflow of capital for an industry 100 percent reliant on imports. Investing in road networks and improvements in order to more efficiently distribute indigenous crops throughout the country and, thus, increasing farm-cooperative proceeds. This multi-impact focus, which looks at not just economic improvements, but also the impact of those changes to lifestyle and well-being, is webbed throughout all governmental policy choices.

The government of Bhutan has proposed that the Sustainable Development Goals of global organizations such as the UN include a measurement of well-being and happiness. Bhutan seems to understand that they alone cannot achieve the vision of GNH and have embraced the path of educating the global community on their vision. While there are no indications this would be an easy or clear path, it is certainly a game-changing concept that offers an alternative to globalization.

References

Alkire, S. 2015. *Well-being, Happiness, and Public Policy.* The Centre for Bhutan Studies & GNH Research.

GNHC. 1999. *Seventh Five Year Plan (1992–1997): Main Document.* Thimphu: Royal Government of Bhutan.

NDP Steering Committee and Secretariat. 2013. *Happiness: Towards a New Development Paradigm.* Report of the Kingdom of Bhutan; Royal Government of Bhutan.

United Nations. 2012. *Defining a New Economic Paradigm: The Report of the High-Level meeting on wellbeing and happiness.* New York: United Nation.

Ura, K., S. Alkire, T. Zangmo, and K. Wangdi. 2015. *Provisional Finding of 2015 GNH Survey.* Centre for Bhutan Studies & GNH Research.

Verma, R., and K. Ura. 2015. "Gender Differences in Gross National Happiness in Bhutan: Analysis of GNH". *Special Issue Journal of Political Ecology on Culture, Power, Degrowth.* 2015 International GNH Conference: From Philosophy to Praxis and Policy Conference Proceedings. Submitted to the Centre for Bhutan Studies and GNH.

CHAPTER 3

Strategic Globalization Alternative

The Case of Kenya

Abel Kinoti Meru and Mary Wanjiru Kinoti

Introduction

Kenya strides the equator on the eastern coast of Africa, bordering Uganda, Tanzania, South Sudan, Ethiopia, and Somali and is the 49th largest country in the world covering a total surface area of 591, 971 square kilometers, with a total population of over 46 million. According to the Kenya National Bureau of Statistics (KNBS) Economic Survey 2017, Kenya's economy expanded by 5.8 percent in 2016 compared to Sub-Saharan Africa's average growth rate of 1.5 percent, maintaining an upward trajectory for more than a decade. After debasing her economy in 2014, Kenya earned the first status of a lower-middle-income economy in East Africa and was ranked among the top 10 economies in Africa.

Kenya, like many African countries, passed through times of purely African traditional practices, British colonial rule (circa 1900s to early 1960s), self-independence (early 1960s to date), Africanization policy (1960s and 1970s), structural adjustment programs (1990s) to the globalization wave that may fully explain the country's socio economic growth and development as its unique positioning within the region. The African traditions embedded strong social cultural institution structures, and the British era paved way for conventional means of livelihood, independence instituted local ownership, while structural adjustment programs addressed sustainability issues.

In spite of the onslaught of globalization on local socio economic activities, locally owned (social) enterprises have maintained a strong foothold within and outside the country albeit invisible. This is attributable to several embedded local, national, and international factors that have played a pivotal role in the growth and development of the economy. Notable among them are home-grown digital solutions, deep-rooted cooperative movements, coupled with growth of savings and credit cooperatives (SACCOs), tea and coffee, the cut flower industry (floriculture), sustainable tourism, export processing zone, regional economic integration, Kenya Airways, and Vision 2030 regional flagship projects.

By positioning along these (social) entrepreneurial lines, Kenya has, arguably, withstood international and global turbulence over the years. This chapter delves on these factors, clearly delineating the critical role each has played fostering national, regional, and international economy and finally offers suggestions and recommendations for future growth and development of the country and beyond.

Digital Entrepreneurial Ecosystem

Communications Authority of Kenya (CAK) has played a fundamental role in facilitating seamless access to broadcasting, postal and courier services, telecommunications, multimedia, and electronic commerce. This is evident by the robust growth in use of internet and mobile communications in the recent past. Osiakwan (2017, p. 55) observes that the advent of submarine cables (for instance, TEAMS, SEACOM, EASSy, and LION2) in Kenya and local terrestrial fiber networks (such as NOFBI, KPC, Jamii Telkom, KDN, and Wanachi) increased existing broadband that enhanced the growth of mobile and web applications, enabling establishment of digital enterprises such as mobile money platform, like Mpesa, which today serves as an alternative banking model. He further notes that lower broadband costs and lower smart phone prices increased mobile access and penetration rate to 90 percent (39.8 million subscribers), leading to establishment of vibrant tech hubs, smart offices, incubators, and accelerators that serve as centers of creativity, innovation, and entrepreneurship within the country. Similarly, internet services and mobile money penetration rate reached 85 percent (37.8 million sub-scribers) and 60 percent (26.3 million subscribers), respectively, by the end of June 2016 (Communications 2017, pp. 17–20).

The mobile money transfer services identified in the Communications Authority of Kenya 2015–2016 annual report include individual to individual cash transfers, payment of goods and services, micro savings and credit, payment of utilities, and bank payments and receipts. By the end of 2016, 1.5 billion transactions had been made worth Ksh 3.4 trillion (US $34 billion), close to half of Kenya's 2015 gross domestic product (Mumo 2017, p. 18). Owing to the convenience of mobile money handling, most institutions have adopted mobile financial transactions including disbursement of salaries, payment of government levies, and loan repayments among others, thus enhancing financial inclusivity. As a result, numerous other applications have been developed to cater for diverse fields such as online shopping (Kilimall), farming (mfarm), health (mtiba), buying government bonds (mkiba), and e-taxi hailing services.

The latter made deep inroads since Nairobi City has over 10,000 taxi cabs, raking in approximately Ksh 7.3 billion (US $73 million) per annum, which attracted global and local technology savvy firms. Since the entry of Uber, an e-hailing taxi service started in January 2015, Kenya has witnessed the emergence of two other global applications, Taxify and Monde ride, and rapid development of home-grown taxi e-hailing appli-cations, led by Little Ride, Maramoja, and Dandia (Njanja 2016, p. 19). Little Ride is a partnership between the telecoms giant Safaricom Kenya Limited and Craft Silicon Company, which offers in addition to the ride, free Wi-Fi, diverse payment options, including Mpesa, a loyalty scheme, lady drivers, corporate taxi, and feedback mechanism. The clamor for the sector is huge given the history of high mobile technology penetra-tion rate in the country and ability of local firms to provide home-grown competitive solutions. Though Uber leads with 1,000 signed drivers, it has encountered several concerns with established taxi cabs including tax-related issues, giving local players an upper edge. Bright (2016) notes that entry of global technology firms in emerging markets may trigger greater local competition to offset globalization disruptive onslaught, and the case of Uber and Little Ride cab transit services are good examples.

Entrenched Cooperative Movement

Ranked as the second in Africa and the seventh in the world, Kenya's cooperative movement started as a dairy cooperative in 1908, during the colonial era, and by 1969 there were 1894 registered societies dealing mainly with marketing of dairy produce, cash crops, and procurement of inputs owned and managed by indigenous farmers (Government 2014). By 2014, Kenya was home to 20,000 registered cooperatives societies, with 10 million members, accounting for 40 percent of gross domestic product (Ksh 436 billion equivalent of US $4.4 billion), drawn from national cooperatives, cooperative unions, and primary cooperatives (Cooperative 2014). The Cooperative (2014) report further notes that the cooperative movement serves over 70 percent of the population and has greatly entrenched financial inclusion in Kenya, with urban and rural areas accounting for over 30 percent of gross national savings (Ksh 230 billion/US $2.3 billion), and with over Ksh 184 billion (US $1.8 billion) in credit provisions to members, through SACCOs.

This alternative banking and micro finance institutions model has over 5,628 SACCOs that operate Front Office Service Activities serving over 4 million customers, almost similar to the number of accounts in the modern banking (Cooperative 2014). SACCOs are registered as either non-deposit-taking (under the Ministry of Industry, Trade and Cooperatives) or deposit-taking SACCOs (regulated by Saccos Regulatory Authority—SASRA) that also offer services such as saving accounts, credit cards, and mobile money transfer. The total assets of 177 registered deposit-taking SACCOs by 2015 stood at Ksh 342 billion (US $3.4 billion), which is the largest in Africa, offering better and friendly interest rates compared to conventional commercial banks and micro finance institutions (SASRA 2015).

Within the agribusiness sector, tea, coffee, and milk agriprocessing and marketing cooperative models are very successful in Kenya, though, unlike tea and coffee which are exported, most of the milk is consumed locally. Kenya leads globally in export of black tea, of which 60 percent is handled by Kenya Tea Development Agency (KTDA); the umbrella body is owned by over 560,000 small-scale tea farmers as shareholders, from 67 tea factories spread throughout tea growing areas (KTDA 2017). Chai Bulletin (2017) shows that by end of June 2016, tea had generated Ksh 84 billion in gross revenue (US $840 million) from 1.23 billion kilograms exported mainly to Pakistan, Egypt, UK, UAE, Afghanistan, Sudan, and Russia among others.

International Finance Corporation (IFC) (2014) featured KTDA as all-inclusive business model integrating agriculture extension services, inputs, logistics, financing, processing, and marketing. Small holder farmers with farm size ranging from 0.5 to 3.5 acres plant and pick tea that is delivered, sorted, and weighed at tea buying centers, and then transported by KTDA tracks to the factories for processing, packaging, and marketing (IFC 2014). A mobile phone real-time integrated system is used to track deliveries and make monthly payments and biannual bonus payments (mainly through Mpesa) after deductions of other costs. Seven KTDA subsidiaries are involved in packaging (Kenya Tea Packers), insurance (Majani Insurance Brokers), micro finance (Green Fedha), power generation (KTDA Power Company), machinery (Tea Machinery and Engineering Company), and social responsibility under KTDA foundation (KTDA 2017). Tea production tremendously improved over the years surpassing coffee which was the leading foreign exchange earner in 1970s, though modeled along the cooperative model, partly due to fluctuating international market prices.

Coffee Growing

Kenya is ranked the 20th producer of fine Arabica coffee with high aroma in the world, despite suffering from depressed market prices since early1980s that saw predominantly small-scale coffee farmers abandon production. In spite of the setback, with improved global market prices coupled with several local and international measures put in place, the sector is set to recover the lost glory. In 2016, coffee production increased by 10.8 percent to 46.1 thousand tonnes from 38.4 thousand tonnes in the previous year, of which 45. 3 thousand tonnes, valued at Ksh 21.4 billion

(US $21 million), was exported (KNBS 2017). Kenya is the main coffee logistics hub for East Africa, and Kenyan coffee is highly sought for blending and in specialty markets, with export market destinations led by Germany, followed by USA, Belgium, Sweden, and Finland (GAIN 2017). With increased domestic roasting and local consumption of coffee and sprouting coffee houses (such as Java house) in all major cities in Kenya, exporting branded coffee can carve a niche in the global field, which can rival export of cut flowers (floriculture).

Vibrant Floriculture Industry

Kenya's market share of cut flowers mainly exported to the European Union stood at 38 percent, worth approximately US $700 million, and is expected to grow globally by 5 percent over the next 5 years or so (KFC 2017). Kenya's cut flower competes favorably with Netherlands, Columbia, Ecuador, and Ethiopia, which are the top flower producers in the world despite being flown over 9,000 miles to the markets. With improved trading relations with the east and an opportunity to export directly by air to the US market by end of 2018, Kenya's global cut flower market share will no doubt improve significantly. By end of 2016, there were over 150 registered flower farms with land sizes measuring 0.25 acres to 230 hectares and a workforce of 100,000 employees, impacting over 2 million livelihoods (Riungu 2016). The growth in the sector is attributable to favorable weather conditions, use of hydroponic farming (utilizing pumice instead of soil or sand), geothermal heated green houses, drip irrigation, water management, and energy conservation systems unparalleled globally, hence the tag "grown under the sun" with minimal carbon emissions (Riungu 2016). Interestingly some flower farms such as Oserian farm double as nature and wildlife conservancy areas targeting the tourism sector.

Sustainable Tourism and Hospitality

After agriculture, tourism is the second biggest foreign exchange earner in Kenya. Over the years, millions of visitors set safari (journey) to experience Kenya's natural beauty, witness spectacular wildlife, and engage with hospitable local communities. The wildebeest migration, which is the 7th new wonder of the world, game drives, Great Rift Valley, pristine sandy warm beaches, snowcapped mountain, hot geysers, and beautiful hotels and eco-lodges offer the best attractions. KNBS (2017, pp. 207–212) Economic Survey reports that the tourism sector earned Ksh 99. 7 billion (US $997 million) in 2016 with over 1.3 million tourist arrivals, of whom 71.9 percent were on holiday, mainly, from UK, USA, Germany, India, and Scandinavian countries.

Export Processing Zone

An export processing zone authority was formed in 1990 to spearhead the promotion and growth of export-oriented investments destined for Africa, Europe, and America. By the end of 2016, Kenya had 65 designated export processing zones, 3 of which were publicly owned, hosting 91 enterprises with a total sale of Ksh 68.7 billion (US $68 million), employing over 52,000 workers (KNBS 2017). The report further observes that the Africa Growth Opportunities Act (AGOA), a US government initiative dealing with garments and apparel, took the lion's share of the exports with sales of Ksh 35.2 billion (US $35 million) and employed over 42,000 workers. The government intends to increase Export Processing Zone (EPZ) local sales quota by 40 percent from the existing 20 percent to spur employ-ment, revive the textile industry, and reduce imports of new and second hand garments (Igadwah 2017, p. 1). According to Construction News Online (2017), Chinese companies, CIFAL International Ltd and China International Investment, are building a Sino-Africa incubation park in the EPZ at a cost of Ksh 20 billion (US $200 million) to support African companies develop technology, manufacturing, processing, and value added services to enhance competitiveness of local products and services nationally, regionally, and at the global arena.

Regional Market Integration

Kenya being the largest economy in East Africa plays a significant role within and outside the East African Community (EAC). Initially, formed in 1967, the EAC is home to over 155 million people and the second largest economic integration block in Africa with a combined gross domestic product of US $150 billion and growth rates averaging over 5 percent per annum. The regional commonalities driving trade and investment include sociocultural factors (language), economic factors (shared infrastructure), institutional factors (common market), human factors (cross border mobility), and geographical conditions (some land-locked countries).

Fdi Intelligence (2015) report indicated that by 2015 notable Kenyan firms' investments projects, within and outside the region, excluding retail sector, included Kenya Commercial Bank with 34 projects; Equity Bank with 23 projects; Diamond Trust Bank with 17 projects; Commercial Bank of Africa, Harleys, Sameer group, Kenol Kobil group each with five projects; and Crown Berger with four projects among others. Sameer group had created the highest number of jobs (893), while KenolKobil had the highest capital investment of US $3,282.4. It is imperative to note that most of the companies have an annual turnover ranging from US $100 million to US $1 billion (Fdi intelligence 2015). Thus, Kenyan firms, particularly in the financial sector, have strong presence and dominance within East Africa.

Kenya Airways: The Pride of Africa

The aviation industry in Kenya contributes approximately 10 percent of the gross domestic product and has played a significant role in driving the country's competitiveness as a regional hub over decades. Kenya Airways started in 1977 after disbandment of East Africa Airways, which operated directly under the original EAC, two decades ago leveraged on KLM's competitiveness in the global arena to emerge as Africa's best airline that has so far won international accolades like Africa's leading airline business class in the world travel awards 2015 and Kenya Airways cargo as African cargo airline of the year award 2015 (Kenya Airways 2017a). Kenya Airways, a public listed company, employs over 4,000 people directly and offers employment opportunities to over 140,000 others indirectly. Being a member of the Sky Team alliance with 36 modern aircrafts, it flies over 4 million passengers annually to 42 African destinations and

11 destinations out of Africa under the banner connecting Africa to the world and the world to Africa (Kenya Airways 2017b).

Vision 2030 Flagship Projects

Under the Vision 2030 flagship projects, the government intends to link Sothern Sudan and Ethiopia through Lamu Port, on the East Africa coast in an infrastructural project dubbed Lamu Port Southern Sudan Ethiopia Transport corridor (LAPSSET). The project aims to provide interregional railway, highway, oil pipeline, airport, and fiber optical cables, which is expected to cost Ksh 2.4 trillion (US $240 billion) on the Kenyan side alone (LAPSSET 2016). The corridor is expected to pass through Central African Republic to Doula on the West Africa coast. Already substantial deposits of crude oil have been discovered in Northern Kenya, strengthening the prioritization of the project.

Another flagship project linking coastal city of Mombasa to Nairobi, to Kisumu, then Kampala (Uganda) to Kigali (Rwanda) and hopefully to Democratic Republic of Congo with standard gauge railway line is on course. Phase 1 of the project from Mombasa to Nairobi was commissioned on June 1, 2017, at a cost of Ksh 327 billion (US $3.8 billion). The Kenyan side of the project is expected to cost Ksh 1 trillion, approximately US $10 billion (Vision 2030 2017). It is widely believed that once completed the project will enhance Kenya's competitiveness in the region.

Suggestions and Recommendations

Despite the socio economic threat posed by globalization, it is clear from the aforesaid that analysis of country or regional specific factors would yield strategic globalization alternatives similar to the Kenyan situation, which are propelling economic growth and prosperity. The unprecedented growth and development of the digital economy has tilted money and financial markets landscape, including tapping the bottom of the pyramid segment as evidenced by exponential growth of Mpesa mobile money transactions. Other notable areas include logistical (Little Ride) and mobile farming solutions that enhance efficiency in the demand and supply of factors of production resulting in improved profitability.

Similarly, over years, natural resource endowments have offered different economies' comparative advantages that have uniquely positioned them both regionally and internationally as demonstrated by growing of tea, cut flowers, coffee, and nature and wildlife conservation in Kenya. This applies also for countries with a vantage geographical position like Kenya serving several landlocked countries (Uganda, Rwanda, Burundi, Southern Sudan, and, to some extent, Central Africa Republic), including parts of Northern Tanzania, Eastern Democratic Republic of Congo, and Southern Ethiopia.

All these factors explain the rationale for the rapid growth and development of regional markets, Kenyan firms, and flagships projects. Thus, if these strategic globalization alternatives are sustained and given the rapid economic and population growth in Africa and beyond, then Kenya's unglobalized economic sectors could, within the next 5 years, help fully digitize most monetary and nonmonetary transactions, attain a 100 percent financial inclusivity, entrench social entrepreneurial culture, intensify agricultural development, and expand economic growth rate by double digit that is needed to achieve a middle-income economic status by the year 2030 as predicted in Kenya's economic blueprints. This will no doubt pose unprecedented challenges to corporate executives, entrepreneurs, and policy makers. Business executives ought to invest heavily in information technology infrastructure to support seamless operations linking businesses with the ultimate consumers, while, on the other hand, entrepreneurs must embrace all-inclusive social business models and the policy makers should promote a conducive working environment.

Nonetheless, these hitherto Kenyan home-grown solutions are widely embraced or adopted within the continent and beyond. Safaricom (Mpesa) is eyeing expansion into other African countries, beginning with the East African market. Similarly, Little Ride taxi hailing app intends to tap the West African market by early next year. Lastly, by mid-2018 Kenya Airways will make its maiden flight to the US market, exploiting further multilateral agreements, including the AGOA and American tourists.

References

Bright, J. 2016. "Kenya Is Giving Globalization an African Twist and It Is Paying Off". *World Economic Forum.* https://www.weforum.org/agenda/2016/10

/kenya-is-giving-globalization-an-african-twist-and-it-s-paying-off/ (accessed June 17, 2017).

Chai Bulletin. 2017. "Chai Bulletin Newsletter April–June, 2017". http://www.ktdateas.com/pdfdocuments/ChaiBulletins/Final%20Newsletter%20email%20version.pdf (accessed June15, 2017).

Communications Authority of Kenya. 2017. "Annual Report 2015–2016 Financial Year". http://ca.go.ke/images//downloads/PUBLICATIONS/ANNUALREPORTS/Annual%20Report%20for%20the%20Financial%20Year%202015-2016.pdf (accessed June 13, 2017).

Construction News Online. 2017. " Chinese Company Breaks Ground on US 200mn Industrial Park in Nairobi". January 6, 2017. https://constructionreviewonline.com/2017/01/chinese-company-breaks-ground-on-us200mn-industrial-park-in-nairobi/ (accessed June 15, 2017).

Cooperative Alliance of Kenya. 2014. "Cooperative Alliance of Kenya, About Us". http://www.cak.coop/about-us.html/ (accessed June 5, 2017).

Fdi Intelligence. 2015. "FDI Between Inter East Africa Countries. Cross Border Investment Monitor". London: Financial Times Limited. www.fdiintellingence.com

GAIN. 2017. "2017 Kenya Coffee Report". *USDA Foreign Agricultural Services*. https://gain.fas.usda.gov/Recent%20GAIN%20Publications/Coffee%20Annual_Nairobi_Kenya_5-15-2017.pdf (accessed June, 17, 2017).

Government of Kenya. 2014. "History and Organization of Cooperative Development and Marketing Sub Sector." Nairobi: *Ministry of Industrialization and Enterprise Development*. http://www.industrialization.go.ke/index.php/downloads/123-history-and-organization-of-cooperative-development-and-marketing-sub-sector-in-kenya/ (accessed June 3, 2017).

Riungu, C. 2016. "The Kenya Flower Industry at a Glance". *Hortinews*, June, 2016. Nairobi: Karuri Ventures Limited.

IFC. 2014. "IFC Inclusive Business Company Profile", *Kenya Tea Development Agency Limited*. https://www.ifc.org/wps/wcm/connect/7a370e68-cbe5-4c2a-96e5-92d6fcadf57d/KTDA.pdf?MOD=AJPERES (accessed June 15, 2017).

Igadwah, L. 2017. "EPZ Firms Local Sales Raised by 40 Percent". *Business Daily*, May 1, 2017. http://www.businessdailyafrica.com/news/EPZ-firms--local-sales-quota-raised-to-40pc/539546-3910518-gui6okz/index.html/ (accessed June 19, 2017).

Kenya Airways. 2017a. "History of Kenya Airways". https://www.kenya-airways.com/about-us/corporate-profile/our-history/en/ (accessed June 17, 2017).

Kenya Airways. 2017b. "KQ on Course to Secure Its Future." https://www.kenya-airways.com/about-us/media-room-press-release/kq-on-course-to-secure-its-future/ (accessed June 17, 2017).

KFC. 2017. "Floriculture in Kenya". http://kenyaflowercouncil.org/?page_id=92 (accessed June 17, 2017).

KNBS. 2017. "Economy Survey 2017". Nairobi: KNBS. https://www.knbs.or.ke/download/economic-survey-2017/ (accessed June 15, 2017).

KTDA. 2017. "Our Background". http://www.ktdateas.com/index.php/about-us/our-background.html/ (accessed June 15, 2017).

LAPSSET. 2016. "Brief on LAPSSET Corridor Project, July 2016". Nairobi: LAPSSET Corridor Development Authority. www.vision2030.go.ke (accessed June 17, 2017).

Mumo, M. 2017. "Safaricom to Re-launch its Revenue Stream". *Daily Nation*, March 18, 2017. http://www.nation.co.ke/news/Safaricom-to-relaunch-its-revenue-stream-M-Pesa/1056-3853936-m858wuz/index.html/ (accessed June 15, 2017).

Njanja, A. 2016. "Battle for e-hailing Market Share Moves to Personalized Services". *Business Daily*, October 19, 2016. http://www.businessdailyafrica.com/Battle-for-Kenya-e-hailing-market-share-moves-to-services/1248928-3422624-o2152w/index.html/ (accessed June 6, 2017).

Osikakwan, E.M.K. "The KINGS of Africa's Digital Economy". in Ndemo, B., and Weiss, T. (eds.) *Digital Kenya: An Entrepreneurial Revolution in the Making*. London: Palgrave Macmillan, p. 55.

SASRA. 2015. "The SACCO Supervision Report, 2015". Nairobi: The Sacco Societies Regulatory Authority. https://www.sasra.go.ke/index.php/resources/sacco-supervision-reports/category/11-sacco-supervision-reports#.WU52u-uGPIU (accessed June 5, 2017).

Vision 2030. 2017. New Dawn for Kenya as Standard Gauge Railway Rolls Out Service. http://www.vision2030.go.ke/549/new-dawn-for-kenya-as-standard-gauge-railway-rolls-out-services/ (accessed June 5, 10, 2017).

CHAPTER 4

The Alternative of Pursuing Localization before Globalization

The Case of the City of Ferguson and International Media

Shelly Daly

Introduction

In 2014, the whole world came to know the town of Ferguson. Where it was within the realm of the continental United States, which state the town could be found in, what geographic region it inhabited were side-bars that were rarely mentioned and information that was not relevant to most news reports. Ferguson, a town in the North County region of the state of Missouri, just minutes from Illinois and the Mississippi River, was not in need of any further nomenclature. It would be known by one word, the city name, on lips around the world.

A man had been shot by a police officer and if the world could not readily name the officer, the name of the dead man was quickly known and repeated and eulogized. Information about this shooting went viral. That is not to say the information was accurate or well-founded or hastily thrown together. Not even the passage of 3 years has clarified the information for some people. Shootings happen daily in every city in the United States. Populaces large and small, rich and poor, have stories of gun violence to tell.

The following pages are not attempting to discern the events, role of the justice system or world media, nor the guilt or innocence of any person or group. The analysis that follows is an attempt to look at alternative measures for Ferguson in the aftermath of global infamy. Healing has come slowly (some would say not at all) and rebuilding has been painstaking. The case of the tiny city of Ferguson offers us the ability to analyze and observe their restructuring and future in light of the globally noticed, reported, and talked about events that have brought major focus on an otherwise unnoticed and remedial, if not typical, mid-western town.

The Event: The Catalyst to Global Notoriety

Just before noon on an August day in 2014, two teenagers living in Ferguson, Missouri left a liquor store having stolen Cigarillos. Alerted to the theft and absorbing the description of the thieves, a police officer quickly spots the men on a street not far from the store. The robber, although not carrying a weapon, proceeded to assault the police officer physically and was shot and killed. While some called this murder, a grand jury found the officer acted in self-defense and the incident was finished in the court of law. The court of opinion, media scrutiny, and world attention would dispute the incidents and potential factors for days, months, weeks, and years. The only clear-cut aspect of the incident seemed to be that the officer was white and the dead man was black.

"Ferguson Shooting" was repeated in the local media and by global outlets in small and large cities around the globe. Protests began immediately and focused on the incident and the role played by law officers. The officer's exoneration only seemed to fuel those who wanted, needed, and pursued a voice of anger, outrage, and persecution. The US Department of Justice Statistics show that more than 90 percent of people living in and arrested in Ferguson were African-Americans and 93 percent of police officers stationed in the city were white (McGraugh and Rosenfeld 2015). Wilson and Wilson (2015) in the *Journal of Critical Incidents* quote a 20 percent poverty rate in Ferguson. Demonstrations and protests spread throughout the United States as the world watched. The now readily-used slogan "Black lives matter" made a daily appearance in news feeds and on election-style front lawn signs. Protests often turned violent, and in Ferguson itself, it resulted in mass destruction of property, arson, and looting. Preexisting tensions in the predominantly black city easily erupted (Buchanan 2014) and fed the fire of social unrest far beyond the borders of Ferguson.

Prior to 1970, Ferguson was comprised of an almost entire white population. The population change happened quickly and property values fell and real estate blight grew. Despite a racially changing populace, Sanchez (2014) reports that of the 53 police officers in the city of Ferguson, only three were African-American. The world absorbed the racial tension from afar, but easily fed the flames and increased the glare.

The Immediate Aftermath

Globalization involves exchange of information, goods, services, culture, and people across the borders and oceans of the world. Just as the good things spread, so do the bad things. While most of the world enjoys the idea of 4G phone service while traveling to remote locations, this ease of technological access also aides and abets those who wish to cause harm or acts of terror. Ferguson became a word, a single word, that divided the nation and world viewers on the basis of race and culture, and the world watched. News of the event flooded stations in Lund, Montreal, Beijing, and Thimphu. Bonilla and Rosa (2015) state that "during the initial week of protests, over 3.6 million posts appeared on Twitter documenting and reflecting on the emerging details surrounding Michael Brown's death; by the end of the month, '#Ferguson' had appeared more than eight million times on the Twitter platform."

There were immediate and desperate attempts to clean up and rebuild Ferguson in the wake of the riots, looting, and fires that protestors set. The St. Louis Economic Development Partnership prepared a marketing campaign to boost Ferguson's post-shooting image. Citizens, elected officials, outsiders, and corporations found ways to help clean up physical damage, organize small businesses with rebuilding, and jump-start future development and entrepreneurial investing. "For us, this is an opportunity to do better than we have done," said Mr. Jerome Jenkins who is the owner of Cathy's Kitchen in Ferguson, "The world will be watching" (Corley 2015).

Moving Forward: An Alternative to the Global Spotlight

Avoiding Globalization's Lure: Rebuilding and the Local Economy

Globalization refers to "the widening set of interdependent relationships among people from different parts of the world that happen to be divided into nations" (Daniels et al. 2015). Studies have shown that globalization increases vulnerability and insecurity (Gaur 2015). Mutual dependence has many benefits but, often times, it decreases the need for a nation or city or region to be self-sufficient, whether by choice, ease of lifestyle choice, or even short-sightedness. Ferguson, the city, the topic, the media coverage, the police response, and the rebuilding are all intricately tied to the forces of globalization due to the global awareness and reporting of the event. While globalization fosters integration among countries, states, and people, it can and does contribute to inequality in some cases. Globalization fosters competitiveness, and competition dictates the role of a winner and loser. For the low-income town of Ferguson, with its high poverty rate, the local government and citizens could not and are not effectively competing against the global news coverage and distinct portrayal of events. Ferguson seems to be losing the "image" game when it comes to reports and newscasts. Daniels (2015) defines sovereignty as "freedom to act locally and without externally imposed restrictions." Ferguson has lost its sovereignability to act in its own best interest. "Social unrest can have a lasting negative impact on a local economy in a way that's much more persistent than even a natural disaster" (Simon et al. 2016). After rioting, by contrast, it is much harder to rebuild confidence and community trust among frightened business owners or to convince new employers to move in (Poppick 2016).

"Our society is so interconnected today with technology and media at the forefront of every newsworthy story that it is now almost impossible to isolate them from each other" (Weigel and Heikkinen 2007, p. 15). Often times, this overload of technology access serves to feed fear, chaos, and misinformation. The world seems to obsess on the drama, and the repeated showing of horrific events and the ability to view the event repeatedly from various angles serve to instill not only increased fear and discomfort but a skewed and excessive view of the event. Global citizens tend to become so reliant on immediate access to information and technology that a balanced world view is lost. People form quick and immediate impressions, and these impressions become opinions and judgments that are repeated without proper reflection and balance against fuller information. Often times, hysteria, chaos, and fear are created. By the time proper investigative forces and reporting occur, the mass of population has moved on to the next dramatic event, and there is no ability to correct, rectify, or revisit earlier opinions. "There is some evidence that growth in globalization goes hand in hand not only with increased insecurity about jobs and social status but also with costly social unrest" (Daniels et al. 2015, p. 17).

The Option of Isolation

Isolation of communities' affairs can be very good in time of turmoil because while the surrounding areas may be falling apart, those that implement isolation may not be as vulnerable to falling apart (Isolation vs. Globalization; par. 12). "The social aspect of sustainability examines the social relationships and interactions that satisfy human needs of the present without compromising the needs of future generations" (Daniels 2015, p. 414). Social sustainability and isolation may allow Ferguson to foster relationships among its citizens, police, governing forces, and business people. These relationships are damaged and strained, and many businesses have failed to rebuild due to lack of internal support or assistance. Many business owners and residents report first-hand accounts of destruction of property and fire setting that took place by protestors from outside of Ferguson entering the city borders. Integration and reliance on each other may rebuild the town and the relationships to a point that is stronger and sustainable for the long term.

The fast and significant racial change of 1970s that Ferguson created was social disparities between its citizens. The idea of social sustainability also encompasses human rights and justice, which is an area that the global media and the residents of Ferguson feel deeply about addressing. "Ferguson needs a city revitalization process that is grounded not in a single short-term improvement, but in systemic change. A systemic change capable of sustaining improvement over time not only in a narrow sphere but with a broader vision of a just city" (Mallach, 2013, p. 9).

The US Department of State Official Blog mentioned this: "We wish that the tragic events in Ferguson hadn't happened. But if other governments responded to similar events with the same determination to protect their citizens' rights and freedoms, the world would be a better place" (Malinowski 2014, par. 12). While views may differ on human rights issues or abuses within Ferguson, all sides seem to agree that it is a paramount issue in the rebuilding of the city. Allowing the city to address its own unique identity, history, class makeup, and rebuild in a way that is long term and sustainable can only happen if each citizen, elected official, and business person embraces the plan. Isolating and insulating themselves from undue influence and negative global media attention will allow those most affected by and living in the situation to rebuild in a way that matches their needs.

Isolation also empowers those directly living in and rebuilding Ferguson. Koper, Woods, and Isom (2016) found that empowerment of the people in a community can regenerate the economy and social life of that community, and most would agree that Ferguson needs a quick, sustained regeneration. Empowerment would also come through employment within the city by its residents. A work force made up of neighbors would offer a level of invested interest in the long -term viability of any rebuilding.

"The peoples and governments of island nation-states appear to use isolation as a jurisdictional resource to address the challenges of economic globalization" (Stratford 2006). Ferguson, viewed as an island, isolating itself from outside challenges and distractions, could rebuild in its own image, owning the good and bad that results from its new city.

Order from Disorder

"Public interactions have a high chance to be observed by others and always affect reputation. Private interactions have a lower chance to be observed and only occasionally affect reputation . . . We observe the competition between 'honest' and 'hypocritical' strategies. The former cooperate both in public and in private. The later cooperate in public, where many others are watching, but try to get away with defection in private situations. The hypocritical idea is that in private situations it does not pay-off to cooperate, because there is a good chance that nobody will notice it" (Ohtsuki et al. 2015, p. 1). Global attention has forced Ferguson's every move and nuance to be over-evaluated in the public eye. The stress and pressure of constant and often negative media attention would naturally lead to an inconsistency in stated plans, desires, and goals by many involved in rebuilding. The immediacy of time in media news feeds does not allow for private reflection among those closest to the incident and rebuilding efforts.

"The phenomenon is seen in research showing that after observing others violate social norms or rules, individuals are more likely to violate other norms or rules; this is the spreading of disorder" (Ziqing and Rongjun 2016, p. 2). Often the mass protests in and about Ferguson erupted in violence against persons and property. Complaints from the citizens of Ferguson were repeated often that much of the mass destruction of property within city borders was taking place by those that did not reside in Ferguson itself. People traveled a great distance to take part in the protests, and few of these protests were calm or peaceful.

"Respect for human rights creates an environment conducive to the development of human capital and encourages a more open, well-trained, and economically efficient society" (Blanton and Blanton 2007). While many see the "Black Lives Matter" movement as a means for, catalyst, and impetus toward human rights, Ferguson would benefit by reducing over-reliance on this movement. The movement needs to be separate from the rebuilding of Ferguson; each has its own agenda and vast amount of work to do; the movement also gives outsiders with a lack of knowledge and cultural awareness about the city the ability to have influence in Ferguson and possibly advance a different agenda than that necessarily of interest to the residents of the city. The long -term goal is to give Ferguson a comparative advantage in reconstructing its city in its desired image, industry, and government make up.

A report by Starr and Adams (2003) called *The Global Fight for Local Autonomy* states that advocates of local-scale economies encourage consumers to support local producers and consumers who find this process rewarding and positive. Ferguson leaders would benefit from this rebuilding from within not just financially, but also through civic pride and mental ownership of the future. Globalization poses a huge threat to sovereignty, and we often forget that city and town sovereignty is just as relevant as national sovereignty. Global pressure from media, interest groups, or leadership will threaten the ability of this city to rebuild in an image that its citizens can culturally own and recognize.

Many people readily associate globalization with unfair social outcomes and oppose it precisely for this reason; "The anti-globalization movement builds on the feeling that prevailing patterns of trading relations and income distribution are unjust and morally reprehensible" and global influence is frequently opposed due to this bent toward unfair social outcomes (Lubker 2004, p. 98). This effect is often exacerbated for poor and low-income individuals and families whose social problems and situations are unique to their society (Pyles 2010).

Dr. Rangarajan (2006) of the Economic Advisory Council of New Delhi is leery of the outcomes of globalization as he believes it can further income inequality. Struggling and low-income cities similar to Ferguson are often pressured to provide multinational companies tax incentives to build stores in their communities. The "Walmart Effect," where multinationals move in at the expense of indigenous businesses, has not offered stability or growth or rebuilding to the communities where small-scale businesses are forced close. Thus, one could argue for the need to avoid "big business" as a means of bringing order after this chaotic 3 years of turmoil if Ferguson would like to maintain some aspects of its former identity and culture.

Concluding Thoughts

Globalization's allure, promise, and possibilities may be the future for tiny Ferguson, but there is a solid argument to be made in rebuilding without, and away from, further global media scrutiny. While the point is not to argue that the world never had a role or a say in the events of August 2014, it is more in speaking to the current ability and alternative for Ferguson, Missouri to move forward at its own pace, style, and culturally idiosyncratic way. The ability and choice to "go global" must reside within the citizenry and law-makers of this small city, if, and when, they chose and not because it is forced upon them from without.

Models of globalization offer good examples and protocols for Ferguson as they traverse this decision. Just as countries and governments have, for centuries, used the tide of globalization to insulate or spread their cultural identity, so too can this Missouri community use these examples to make the decision that fits their cultural identity and growth plan.

Note: *With special thanks to the fall 1, 2016 IBO MBA class at Lindenwood University for their thoughts on this topic and their willingness to discuss and investigate alternatives to globalization.*

References

Blanton, S.L., and R.G. Blanton. 2007. "What Attracts Foreign Investors? An Examination of Human Rights and Foreign Direct Investment." *The Journal of Politics* 69, no. 1, pp. 143–155.

Bonilla, Y., and J. Rosa. 2015. "#Ferguson: Digital Protest, Hashtag Ethnography, and the Racial Politics of Social Media in the United States." *American Ethnologist* 42, no. 1, pp. 4–17. Academic Search Complete. Web. September 11, 2016.

Buchanan L., and F. Fessenden. 2014. "What Happened in Ferguson?", *The New York Times*, Web. September 7, 2016. http://www.nytimes.com /interactive/2014/08/13/us/ferguson-missouri-town-under-siege-after-police-shooting.html.

Corley, C. 2015. "Ferguson Businesses Struggle to Rebuild Post-Riots." *All Things Considered* (NPR), Newspaper Source, Web. September 12, 2016.

Daniels J.R., H. Lee, and D. Sullivan. 2015. *International Business Environments and Operations.* 15th ed. Harlow: Pearson.

Gaur, A. 2015. "Impact of Globalization on Trade and Employment", *International Journal of Multidisciplinary Approach & Studies.* http://eds.a.ebscohost.com /ehost/pdfviewer/pdfviewer?sid=d871886e-b456-40ae-bbb4-d535932b19a d%40sessionmgr4006&vid=3&hid=4213.

"Isolation Vs. Globalization." Weebly, n.d. Web. http://ivsg.weebly.com/.

Koper, C.S., D.J. Woods, and D. Isom. 2016. "Evaluating a Police-Led Community Initiative to Reduce Gun Violence in St. Louis." *Police Quarterly* 19.2 115–149. Academic Search Complete. Web. September 10, 2016.

Lubker, M. 2004. "Globalization and perceptions of social inequality." *International Labour Review* 143, no. 102, pp.91–128.

Malinowski, T. 2014. "Ferguson and International Human Rights." *U.S. Department of State.* U.S. Department of State, Web. September 11, 2016. https://blogs .state.gov/stories/2014/09/09/ferguson-and-international-human-rights.

McGraugh, S.,R. Rosenfeld, and Census Bureau; Missouri State Highway Patrol. 2014. "What happened in Ferguson." *New York Times*. http://www.nytimes.com/interactive/2014/08/13/us/ferguson-missouri-town-under-siege-after-police-shooting.html.

Ohtsuki, H.Y., Y. Iwasa, and M.A. Nowak. 2015. "Reputation Effects in Public and Private Interactions." *PLoS Computational Biology* 11, no. 11, pp. 1–11. Academic Search Elite. Web. September 11, 2016.

Poppick, S. "Can Ferguson Recover? The Lasting Economic Impact of Violent Unrest." *Time*. http://time.com/money/3145128/ferguson-riots-recovery-economic-impact-unrest/ (accessed September 11, 2016).

Pyles, L. 2010. "Global Justice in the Time of Obama: A Call to Organize." *Social Work* 55, no. 1, pp. 90–92.

Rangarajan, C. 2006. "Responding to Globalization: India's Answer." *4th Ramanbhai Patel Memorial Lecture Excellence in Education*.

Sanchez, R. 2014. "Michael Brown Shooting, Protests Highlight Racial Divide." *CNN*. Cable News Network. http://www.cnn.com/2014/08/14/justice/ferguson-missouri-police-community/.

Simon, R., B. Kesling, and L. Josephs. 2015. "In Ferguson, Business Faces Long Road Back." *Wall Street Journal – Eastern Edition*, 15 June 2015, pp. A1+. *Business Source Premier*. Web. September 8, 2016.

Starr, A. and J. Adams 2003. "Anti-globalization: The Global Fight for Local Autonomy." *New Political Science* 25, no. 1.

Stratford, E. 2006. "Isolation As Disability and Resource: Considering Sub-National Island Status in the Constitution of the 'New Tasmania'." *Round Table* 95.386: 575.

Weigel, M., and K. Heikkinen, 2007. "Developing Minds with Digital Media: Habits of Mind in the YouTube Era." *Goodwork Project Report Series*, no.51. http://www.thegoodproject.org/pdf/No-51-Developing-Minds-with-Digital-Media.pdf.

Wilson, C., and S. Wilson. 2015. "A Community Unraveled: Police Shooting in Ferguson, MO." *Journal of Critical Incidents*, pp. 852–855.

Ziqing, Y., and Y. Rongjun, 2016. "The Spreading of Social Energy: How Exposure to Positive and Negative Social News Affects Behavior." *South China Normal University. PLoS One* 11, no. 6, p. e0156062. https://doi.org/10.1371/journal.pone.0156062

SECTION 3

Institutions and Policies

CHAPTER 5

International Financial Institutions (IFIs)

Facilitators or Obstructionists to Globalization?

Diana Heeb Bivona

Following the end of World War II when a greater interdependence among the nations of the world emerged, there was an increased interest among many countries to establish international financial institutions (IFIs). This resulted in the creation of institutions such as the World Bank, the International Monetary Fund (IMF), and the International Finance Corporation (IFC), and later expanded to include multilateral development banks (MDBs), and various other international developmental agencies. The scope and increasing influence of these IFIs have led to their description as "the world's most powerful agents of economic reform" (Halliday and Carruthers 2007).

Researchers have argued that a move toward greater financial integration has promoted income risk sharing and consumption while reducing the volatility of consumption growth (Bekaert et al. 2006). IFIs have played a pivotal role by offering financial support for the economic and social development activities in many countries. Through grants and loans, IFIs have lent on average, between US $30 and $40 billion annually to low- and middle-income countries.

Proponents point to the positive aspects of IFIs' financing such as promoting cooperation, supporting countries in their endeavors to combat poverty, developing infrastructure, and undertaking extensive domestic and market-oriented reforms to better compete in international markets. IFIs also provide important countercyclical support for countries that suffer financial shocks in times of crisis. This is an especially important consideration for developing countries that may have a more difficult time reducing the effects of exogenous shocks like those felt in the most recent global financial crisis or from devastating natural disasters. Often, the financial systems of these countries lack stability and the needed fiscal and monetary policy instruments to ride out such fluctuations to their economic and financial systems (Berensmann and Wolff 2013).

An example can be seen in Grenada following Hurricane Ivan in 2004, which devastated various economic sectors, destroyed physical infrastructure, and eroded the country's macroeconomic fundamentals. The hurricane chipped away at the country's financial health reducing its financial position from a surplus of US $17 million to a deficit of US $54 million as damages from the hurricane amounted to 200 percent of GDP (The Commonwealth 2016). With finances reduced, the large-scale recovery efforts had to be heavily financed by debt from private and public creditors including the World Bank, IMF, and the Caribbean Development Bank (CDB). Still struggling to gain its footing over a decade later, a second more comprehensive round of debt restructuring was required in 2015. Without such resources, the impact of this exogenous shock would have proven more devastating and potentially financially unrecoverable.

Critics suggest that accepting the much-needed financing from IFIs comes with too many strings attached. These strings, known as loan conditions, include such requirements as the privatization of industries, elimination of subsidies, greater financial liberalization, and reduction in salaries for civil servants as defined and on a timetable prescribed by the IFIs. This has resulted in IFIs gaining significant and undue power and influence over the economic development of many emerging and developing markets. It has also resulted in billions of dollars in loan defaults by countries such as Argentina, Greece, Somalia, Sudan, and Zimbabwe to name a few.

IFIs have claimed to be apolitical in their policies, procedures, and decision-making, yet evidence suggests a preference for funding the interests of major shareholders like the United States (Dreher et al. 2009; Kilby 2009; Vreeland and Dreher 2014). This has led to an increase in questions as to how IFIs can pursue their interests and maintain autonomy while serving the objectives set forth by the nations that established them. Increasing conflicts and controversies arising from IFIs suggest such inquiries are warranted.

A recent report by the Independent Evaluation Office (IEO) highlighted some of these concerns. The IMF's independent oversight agency reported on the IMF's failure to notify its board of a significant exception to the Greece bailout package and the allowance of Portugal and Ireland to borrow over 2,000 percent of their allocated quota. Additionally mentioned was the inability of the IEO to locate important documents and records during its inspections, raising alarms regarding the legitimacy and operational security of the IMF (Evans-Pritchard 2016). The World Bank once again found itself defending against recurring criticisms of putting citizenship ahead of merit when it selected its most recent president. It also drew the ire of critics with its decision to relax environmental and social framework safeguard policies related to its lending practices.

It is not surprising that a certain level of distrust and animosity has arisen among many developing nation members and recipients of aid. Calls to reform the structure and policies of IFIs have thus become more frequent and fevered in pitch. In recent years, IFIs such as the IMF and the World Bank have attempted to make changes taking these concerns and criticisms into account, but opponents argue it is too little too late. Many nation-states are now exploring alternatives such as the creation of regional financial banks and organizations that, while still early in their inception, have begun to challenge the supremacy of traditional IFIs. Challengers include the New Development Bank (NDB) backed by the BRICS (Brazil, Russia, India, China, and South Africa), and discussed later, as well as the Asian Infrastructure Investment Bank (AIIB), initiated by China and jointly founded by 57-member countries throughout Asia and elsewhere.

This raises doubts as to how effective traditional IFIs can be in meeting the challenges of globalization in their current, and some would argue, outdated configurations, operating under objectives that appear to run counter to the advancement of the purpose of globalization. This begs the question, have IFIs become obstructionists instead of facilitators of globalization?

Adding Voices to the Chorus

To begin to answer, a closer look at administrative structural issues of the more well-known IFIs needs to be taken. It is not unrealistic to assume that when joining an international organization, members must give up some sovereign rights in exchange for the benefits of joining. In other words, one must give to receive. However, therein lies a bone of contention with developing nations that contend what they are giving up is disproportionate to the benefits received.

A major criticism leveled at IFIs such as the IMF, and to a lesser extent, the World Bank, is that the emerging and developing nations have long-lacked proportionate representation in the governance of these organizations. Governance tactics undertaken have been questionable, and the concessionary lending terms required are often too restrictive and blind to individual country differences. These criticisms are not unwarranted. Additionally, and some may argue more significantly, the developed and emerging members of IFIs were not involved in creating the rules and governing agreements of the current global economic and financial system in which they must participate. Subsequently, newer members have failed to adopt any accountability when it comes to supporting the IFIs' global frameworks and systems.

The emerging and developing nations now produce one-half of the world's GDP, and by 2017, they are expected to grow to three-fourths (Chari and Henry 2014). Yet, throughout much of the IMF's existence, developing nations have often been lumped together in large voting blocs and assigned a small voting quota resulting in underrepresentation. In 2010, the IMF responded to this concern during the 14th General Review of Quotas by doubling quotas to approximately SDR 478.6 billion and realigning quota shares among members (International Monetary Fund 2016). This resulted in emerging and developing nations receiving a 6 percent increase in quota shares. Unfortunately, the reforms, while proposed in 2010, did not take effect until January 2016, leaving many feeling frustrated and disenfranchised not just at the slow pace of change but also at the small increase in overall quota shares.

Even after the realignment of voting quotas, little appears to have changed. Almost 47 percent of IMF voting power remains in the hands of just nine developed countries with the United States holding 17 percent out of the qualified 85 percent required in voting (Garcia 2016). Given these circumstances, it becomes difficult to argue that organizations such as the IMF are not political, despite outward appearances to maintain an apolitical façade of neutrality.

IFIs such as the IMF have also been criticized for lacking in responsibility and evaluation, harboring monopolistic tendencies, and limiting public participation in its decision-making process. Dominated by the wealthiest industrial countries and the various commercial and financial interests of those countries, many of the policy decisions undertaken have favored the interests of those nations. This is a criticism leveled not just against the IMF, but also against the World Bank. Like the IMF, decisions at the World Bank are made in secret with very little accountability for those decisions apparent. Policy decisions lack transparency, and even though both the IMF and World Bank have taken steps to improve transparency, much more work is still needed (Đonlagić and Kožarić 2010).

As mentioned, IFIs' loans have often come with strings attached, and until recently these strings have included requiring developing nations to conform to tight macroeconomic policies that include deep cuts to public spending, higher interest rates, and tight monetary policy (Hill 2014). Other conditions generally have required the deregulation of sectors protected from local and foreign competition, privatization of state-owned assets, and improved financial reporting from the banking sector. IFIs such as the IMF have viewed these conditions as a necessary step to calming volatile economies by reducing rampant inflation and decreasing government spending and debt, but critics assert these policies can prove damaging (Garcia 2016).

Opponents charged that the "one-size-fits-all" macroeconomic policies that the IFIs such as the IMF have followed are inappropriate for many countries. Not all countries are necessarily suffering from excessive government spending and rapidly rising inflation. For instance, a private-sector debt crisis with deflationary undertones can also be the culprit as was the case during the 1997 Asian crisis (Hill 2014). By following the IMF's strict macroeconomic policies, businesses within countries such as South Korea found themselves struggling to meet short-term debt obligations, potentially contributing to higher corporate default rates. Despite the seemingly good intentions of the IMF and its loan initiatives, implementing such programs often exacerbated rather than calmed a crisis (Stiglitz 2009). It also contributed to further social and economic instability, as well as further inequality (Stiglitz 2009).

It is not a stretch to understand why critics question the legitimacy of IFIs given these actions. Politicized institutions, influenced by large shareholders exerting influence over lending policies, with questionable governance practices, lend to the belief that IFIs have indeed become obstructionists and not facilitators of globalization. It also explains why countries are looking for alternatives to IFIs.

Forging Another Path Forward

The longevity and the track record of IFIs have provided these organizations with a comparative advantage when it comes to mobilizing resources and supporting various projects globally. IFIs, in the past, have contributed to global stability. They have focused on assisting emerging market economies in making rapid progress and in fighting poverty, but global challenges are growing in scope and size. Now, more than ever, the need for good governance, including transparency, public ownership of policy decisions, and the need for partnerships that extend beyond empty promises are essential for success.

While IFIs such as the World Bank and the IMF have provided emerging and developing nations with a source of liquidity many otherwise would not have had access to, the restrictive, "one-size-fits-all" loan program, the underrepresentation found in the governance structure, and the IFIs' slow response to demands for reform have led to frustration and criticism by many of its members. It likely also has served as a catalyst for many members who have decided to take a more proactive role in fostering developmental cooperation and in finding ways to reduce the influence of traditional IFIs.

For developing countries, embracing globalization means opening themselves up to additional risks. Larger developed nations that elect to borrow funds from the IFIs such as Brazil, India, China, and South Africa can better shape the lending and operational policies of IFIs and negotiate loan packages that are not as restrictive. However, the low- and middle-income countries are often reluctant to borrow for large infrastructure projects given the social and environmental "strings" that often come with the IFIs financing packages. Other risks arise as well. Take for example the currency crises and recessions noted in Asia and Latin America, which were spurned by sudden reversals of capital flows from loan recalls by international banks or massive sales of emerging market stocks by international funds.

Developing countries are now pursuing steps to reduce the influence of IFIs such as accumulating international reserves to ensure liquidity during times of crisis. Greater liquidity means less dependence on loans. For example, China's reserves increased from $24.8 billion to $3.3 trillion between 1992 and 2012 while Argentina, Brazil, Mexico, and Peru raised their reserves during the same period from $75 billion to $726 billion (Garcia 2016).

Developing nations have also made repaying IMF loans a priority, understanding that by paying off the loans faster, they would be able to shed the restrictive economic yoke placed on them by IFIs and have the freedom to then make national decisions themselves. Latin American and Caribbean countries did just that as noted by the decline in SDRs for the region between 2004 and 2008. Loans during that time dropped from 49.4 percent to 6.7 percent (Garcia 2016).

Seeking Alternatives

Arising from a frustration with the IFIs has been the increase in regional forums, many of which offer alternative financing options. The New Development Bank (NDB) created by and focused on the BRICS nations is one such example. The institution, started by each member contributing $20 billion, provides financing for infrastructure and development in the founding nations (Garcia 2016). In contrast to the IMF, each member country has equal voting power on the executive board.

The NDB intends to play a significant role in addressing areas it believes IFIs have failed to address, such as improving the international monetary system and infrastructure development. However, the NDB still has a way to go before it can challenge and displace traditional IFIs. The NDB still lacks the capacity to do so, but it has demonstrated a willingness, commitment, and voice to push hard for IFIs to undertake much -needed reforms (Qobo and Soko 2015).

Finally, the slow response to enact reforms on the part of IFIs has allowed some developing nations to increase their political and economic influence globally. China and its South–South Cooperation Model is an example of this phenomenon. China provides non-conditional financial assistance to countries in Africa, Asia, and Latin America and insists its motivation is to only achieve mutual benefit (Garcia 2016). China's model emphasizes an "allies-with-benefits" approach to financing, suggesting that by fostering developmental partnerships for mutual gain, countries can advance economically while still ensuring individual development interests are met (DeHart 2012). To date, China has provided financial assistance to over 93 countries. While the West has viewed China's approach with everything from skepticism to alarm, the fact remains that it has allowed emerging and development markets to access financial aid on competitive terms without the structural conditionality found in IFIs' lending practices (Garcia 2016).

Both China and the NDB serve as examples of nontraditional providers of development assistance that have emerged as alternatives to traditional IFIs' lending. Because of the IFIs' slow response to change needed, some developing nations have effectively taken matters into their hands. They have moved to create innovative financial assistance models that allow for consideration of local circumstances, expectations, and interests (Garcia 2016). This, in turn, has the potential to promote long-term growth in developing nations.

It is still important to point out that while alternative organizations to traditional IFIs are growing, many of these institutions still lack a long-term established track record of success. Furthermore, the focus of many of these entities pertains to a specific group of nations or region. They also do not appear to be suited to address global-level issues and concerns, nor are they free of governance problems of their own. Ultimately, these factors could work against new alternative organizations and reinforce the legitimacy and effectiveness of traditional IFIs (Eichengreen and Woods 2016).

Trust and Cooperation Needed

The lack of trust and cooperation in dealing with the IFIs is significant and cannot be underestimated. International cooperation is critical to further integration and globalization. A quick fix or patchwork of existing IFIs' processes, rules, and regulations will not create the economic and financial integration needed to ensure greater global integration. Without a well-harmonized global system in which all countries participate, a clear understanding and subsequent pathway to a globalized world will remain elusive. Instead, all that will remain will be the prevailing individual country interests, which will ultimately undermine globalization efforts.

Achieving such trust and cooperation will require a variety of international organizations committed to working together as facilitators. However, this may not be within the very nature of traditional IFIs that have long enjoyed a relative uninterrupted period of dominance and governance on the world stage. The idea of sharing that stage with newcomers may prove too challenging. Furthermore, it may not be within the very nature of these organizations' largest and most influential shareholders to allow such a global rebalancing of financial and economic clout needed for further globalization.

A Meeting of the Minds

The political, economic, and social circumstances and goals of nations are often different. In some cases, they diverge rather than converge in a global marketplace making a "one-size-fits-all" approach to solving problems unrealistic. The recent financial crisis of the late 2000s illustrates this as well. After the crisis, developed nations focused efforts on returning their economies to levels of growth seen before the crisis, generating employment, and attempting to address the income inequality gap that had widened (Chari and Henry 2014). In contrast, developing nations such as Bangladesh and Rwanda chose to focus on continuing to consolidate the growth and gains they had made over the last few decades. Their efforts remained intent on reforms in key areas such as infrastructure and labor to maintain those high growth levels (Chari and Henry 2014).

These different objectives mean that each country has different needs and wants. For the developing nations, flexibility and programs that supported its long-term development were a must. When existing IFIs obstructed these objectives, the developing nations took it upon themselves to find alternatives. Thus, one could argue that the role IFIs such as the World Bank and IMF have had in the growth of developing nations has been to motivate these nations to create solutions best suited to their individual long-term growth.

IFIs will become a significant barrier to globalization if they fail to undertake reforms in earnest. There is no doubt that IFIs have performed a substantial role in molding the policies, strategies, and priorities of the emerging and developing countries with which they have worked to date. However, IFIs insistence upon continuing to impose policy conditions, as they relate to such issues as market liberalization and privatization, and stringent rules on macroeconomic stability are significant barriers not easily overcome by countries attempting to invest in their development.

Such actions, while potentially well-intended, are holding the very countries that they propose to assist. When combined with a lack of significant representation on the boards that produce the policies and procedures that impact those countries, the current situation remains tenuous. Globalization stagnates.

The international financial system is still far from integrated, and in turn, globalization remains a work in progress. Further integration though is less an issue of *if* but *when* as it appears irreversible given the costs and difficulty to return to any previous status quo (Mussa 2000). Should IFIs, however, continue to assume an obstructionist position to globalization, the *when* will no doubt remain a tentative date sometime in the distant future.

Consequently, if the move toward greater globalization stalls, the likelihood of a multipolar world in which stronger developed regional powerhouse (China, Russia, Brazil, India, and South Africa) and regional organizations such as the NDB gain greater power and influence increases significantly. Ironically, the effects of such regional dominance may not prove any more beneficial than the idea of globalization does to its advocates. It is not a stretch to envision countries such as the United States, China, and Russia, feeling confident in their geopolitical or economic position as a strong regional player. They may believe themselves to be above international law, and at ease with the idea of circumventing it – an all too familiar scenario. Such a belief could lead various regional economic blocks to adopt their own ways of doing things, which could potentially have a detrimental impact not just on trade and economic issues, but on social issues including poverty and human rights.

Globalization requires a heightened level of empathy and sensitivity. A move toward greater globalization will require greater trust and cooperation among all nations. Conditions are generally lacking not just in IFIs today, but the world in general. The return on investment would make efforts to facilitate trust and cooperation worthwhile.

Globalization can provide emerging and developing nations with several benefits including the development of more stable, better regulated financial systems with open access to credit, a key component of economic growth (Schmukler 2004). Globalization can provide emerging and developing countries with opportunities to combat poverty by increasing their economic growth and build physical infrastructure to promote industry. Globalization also can offer nations and companies with access to much-needed resources and technology and an opportunity to improve the standard of living for its people.

IFIs can play a pivotal role in further facilitating globalization and promoting these benefits. However, whether IFIs are committed to affecting significant change and building that much-needed trust and cooperation remain questionable. Should they instead continue to obstruct the path forward to globalization by refusing to share real power, limit board representation, and favor a "one-size-fits-all" approach to lending, the likelihood of a world marked by multipolarity will increase.

Countries and companies attempting to manage a multipolar world would likely find the world would look and behave differently than the globalized landscape under which they may have been laboring. For instance, instead of working toward a single, unifying framework, more emphasis would be needed on developing multilateral frameworks for regulating cross-border investment. Instead of relying upon the US dollar as the "tried-and-true" international currency of choice, a broader stable of currencies would need to be kept in reserve. Additionally, countries and MNCs alike would likely need to adjust to a reality that is marked by increased geoeconomic competition that would require greater cooperation and a reliance on more well-structured intra-regional trade agreements. But, whether a world marked by increasing multipolarity would prove more beneficial than globalization is a discussion for yet another day.

The role IFIs will play in this evolving global landscape will be defined by its relevance to it. Both the IMF and the World Bank have attempted to remain responsive, albeit slowly, to the changing winds. Over the last few decades, the IMF has redefined its mission and the World Bank has expanded its development mandate; however, calls for the IFIs to change how they approach policy-making and system of aid have not been addressed. Furthermore, the demands for these organizations to be more transparent, accountable, and open have gone largely unanswered.

Several recommendations have been suggested as to how IFIs could remain a relevant actor on the global stage. They have run the gamut ranging from returning to directive basics, i.e., ensuring international financial stability and assisting countries facing balance of payments problems to, as former World Bank employee William Easterly suggested, adopting a "search and discover" approach, where IFIs recognize the unique circumstances found in each country and advocate for policy recommendations tailored specifically to that country's situation.

Today, the IFIs continue to exert sizable influence, particularly over shaping the priorities, strategies, and polices of developing countries. This has largely been because they have been the "only game in town" for developing nations when it has come to securing much-needed financial aid for development. The IFIs sizable influence over these countries markets and monetary policies though may be coming to an end as alternative funding sources such as the New Development Bank (NDB), the African Development Bank (ADB), the Inter-American Bank (IDB), and the AIIB gain standing and influence within their respective regions.

Organizations like these may not yet have the clout and financial resources that the traditional IFIs have, but neither did the World Bank nor IMF when first conceived and operations commenced. Time may, therefore, be the defining factor in the discussion of the relevance of not just the role of these newer regional funding institutions but in the continued significance of IFIs as major global players, and at this point in the discussion, it may well be the foe of IFIs as they exist today.

References

Bekaert, G., C. Harvey, and C. Lundblad. 2006. "Growth Volatility and Financial Liberalization." *Journal of International Money and Finance* 25, pp. 370–403.

Berensmann, K., and P. Wolff. 2013. *The Role of International Financial Institutions in Macroeconomic Crises Improving the Architecture of the World Bank and the IMF for Managing Shocks in Developing Countries.* Bonn: Deutsches Institut fur Entwicklungspolitik.

Chari, A., and P.B. Henry. 2014. "Learning from the Doers: Developing Country Lessons for Advance Economy Growth." *American Economic Review* 104, no. 5, pp. 260–265.

DeHart, M. 2012. "Remodeling the Global Development Landscape: The China Model and South-South Cooperation in Latin America." *Third World Quarterly* 33, no. 7, pp. 1359–1375.

Đonlagić, D., and A. Kožarić. 2010. "Justifications of Criticisms of the International Financial Institutions." *Economic Analysis* LV, no. 186, pp. 115–132.

Dreher, A., J.-E. Sturm, and J.R. Vreeland. 2009. "Development Aid and International Politics: Does Membership on the UN Security Council Influence World Bank Decisions?" *Journal of Development Economics* 88, pp. 1–18. doi:10.1016/j.jdeveco.2008.02.003.

Eichengreen, B., and N. Woods. 2016. "The IMFs Unmet Challenges." *Journal of Economic Perspectives* 30, no. 1, pp. 29–52.

Evans-Pritchard, A. 2016. "IMF Admits Disastrous Love Affair with the Euro and Apologises for the Immolation of Greece." *The Telegraph,* July 29. http://www.telegraph.co.uk/business/2016/07/28/imf-admits-disastrous-love-affair-with-euro-apologises-for-the-i/.

Garcia, G. 2016. "The Rise of the Global South, the IMF and the Future of Law and Development." *Third World Quarterly* 37, no. 2, pp. 191–208.

Halliday, T.C., and B.G. Carruthers. 2007. "The Recursivity of Law: Global Norm Making and National Lawmaking in the Globalization of Corporate Insolvency Regimes." *American Journal of Sociology* 112, no. 4, pp. 1135–1202.

Hill, C. 2014. *Global Business Today.* New York: McGraw-Hill Irwin.

International Monetary Fund. 2016. *How the IMF Makes Decisions.* Washington, D.C.: International Monetary Fund. www.imf.org/external/np/exr/facts/govern.htm.

Kilby, C. 2009. "The Political Economy of Conditionality: An Empirical Analysis of World Bank Loan Disbursements." *Journal of Development Economics* 89, no. 1, 51–61.

Mussa, M. 2000. "Factors Driving Global Economic Integration." *Global Economic Integration: Opportunities and Challenges.* Jackson Hole: Federal Reserve Bank of Kansas City.

Qobo, M., and M. Soko. 2015. "The Rise of Emerging Powers in the Global Development Finance Architecture: The Case of the BRICS and the New Development Bank." *South African Journal of International Affairs* 22, no. 3, p. 277.

Schmukler, S. 2004. *Benefits and Risks of Globalization: Challenges for Developing Countries.* Washington, D.C.: World Bank.

Stiglitz, J. 2009. *Globalization and Its Discontents.* London: A&C Black Publishers, Ltd.

The Commonwealth. 2016. *Countercyclical Financial Instruments.* London: Commonwealth Secretariat. http://thecommonwealth.org/sites/default/files/inline/Countercyclical.PDF.

Vreeland, J., and A. Dreher. 2014. *The Political Economy of the United Nations Security Council: Money and Influence.* Cambridge : Cambridge University Press.

CHAPTER 6

Coping with State-Led Unglobalization

A Historical Analysis of Iran's Petroleum Industry

Alireza Saify, Joobin Ordoobody, and Jasper Hotho

Throughout modern history, Iran has experienced significant waves of antiglobalist and anti-Western sentiments. It is therefore somewhat paradoxical that, over the past decades, the National Iranian Oil Company (NIOC), a state-owned corporation, has emerged as the world's second largest player in the global petroleum industry. In this chapter, we trace the origins of the antiglobal pressures NIOC faces at home and show the deep historical embeddedness of these pressures. Specifically, the chapter aims to describe how the institutional logic of the state gradually came to dominate the petroleum sector in Iran, and show that this process took place well before what is commonly assumed to be the main inflection point for antiglobal sentiments in Iran, the 1979 Islamic Revolution. The sections in this chapter are driven by the following questions: What drove the process of unglobalization and nationalization of Iran's petroleum industry? And how has the sector, and NIOC in particular, been able to grow and function in what is one of the world's most global markets? The answers to these questions are sought through a historical reconstruction of the development of Iran's petroleum industry, based primarily on secondary sources.

The exploration of these questions is partially informed by the institutional logics perspective. Institutional logics are "the socially constructed, historical patterns of material practices, assumptions, values, beliefs, and rules by which individuals produce and reproduce their material subsistence, organize time and space, and provide meaning to their social reality" (Thornton and Ocasio 1999, p. 804). The institutional logics perspective provides a useful lens through which to examine the relationships among institutions and actors in social systems in which different institutions compete (Thornton et al. 2012). In exploring the historical development of Iran's petroleum industry, and the strategies of NIOC to cope with the unglobal developments in the sector, particular attention is placed on the institutional logic of the state, or what Greenwood and colleagues (2010, p. 523) describe as "the basic orientation of the state in securing social and political order."

The chapter contributes to the academic literature by showing shifts in the dominance of different logics over time, and the significance of history for understanding the relationship between NIOC and the institutional context within which it operates. Historical analysis also shows how commercial and technical capabilities gained during previous eras can provide firms with skill sets that allow them to compete globally, even under domestic conditions where strong antiglobal pressures prevail. For practitioners, this chapter reveals that the institutional analyses are not only theoretical matters but insightful guidance for them in order to have a better view of the success or failure of alternative strategies.

NIOC Before the 1979 Revolution

In 1909, the Anglo-Persian Oil Company (APOC), a London-based multinational later renamed as British Petroleum, gained exclusive rights of exploring, extracting, and exporting Iran's oil reserves in exchange for a fairly meager payment to the Iranian government. Between 1909 and 1929, its production volume increased about 23-fold, yet Iran's gains from the arrangement only increased about five-fold. In fact, the APOC paid more in tax to the British government than it paid its Iranian partner (Mohaddes and Pesaran 2013; Kinzer 2003; Ferrier 1982). Another concern was that the oil sector in Iran generated fewer jobs than expected, and that most of the workforce hired locally consisted of unskilled workers (Bamberg 1994). This resulted in dissatisfaction of both the state and public in Iran.

In response, in 1932, Reza Shah, the first monarch of the Pahlavi dynasty, canceled the initial concession given to APOC and in 1933 signed a new agreement in which the method of calculating the revenue of the Iranian partner and its rights were revised and clarified (Mina 2004). The negotiations between the Iranian government and APOC, now named the Anglo-Iranian Oil Company, continued into the 1940s. This lasted until Mohammad Mosaddegh, who enjoyed great public support, became Prime Minister. The oil industry of Iran was nationalized in 1951, and the NIOC was established to regain national control over the oil reserves (Mohaddes and Pesaran 2013).

Prior to nationalization, Iran could set neither its oil price nor its production volume. During that time, the common perception was that Britain controlled the Iranian oil industry and that they helped the Shah to strengthen his reign. Consequently, the Shah was considered as serving British interests and opposed to oil nationalization. The emergence of Mosaddegh united Iranians from different social classes who had been struggling to take back control of Iranian oil reserves and initiated the oil nationalization movement (Gasiorowski 1987; Gasiorowski and Byrne 2004; Keddie 1981). This movement had an anticolonialism nature; for Iranians, the United Kingdom was the symbol of colonialism and AIOC was its executive agency in Iran (Yazdani 2017).

After nationalization of the oil industry, NIOC—an international consortium in which AIOC was merely a member—became responsible for the management of oil in Iran (Fadaee 2012). In August 1953, the government of Mosaddegh was overthrown by a coup by the Shah which was supported by the United Kingdom and the United States. The Americans and British believed that Iranian control over oil would have destructive long-term consequences; oil nationalization not only undermined the interests of Britain but also left the control of oil completely to Iran. Moreover, there was concern that other nations, such as Indonesia, Venezuela, and Iraq, might follow the Iranians in oil nationalization, which effectively would result in a transfer of authority of the international oil market from Western corporations to oil-producing countries

(Abrahamian 2008). However, despite continued American and British influence in Iranian politics, after the coup Iran's oil industry was nationalized nevertheless (Fadaee 2012).

By the end of Mosaddegh's government, negotiations between the new government of Iran and the West began. In 1954, the parties reached an agreement to form a new consortium of eight European and American companies responsible for oil extraction in Iran. British Petroleum, the new name of AIOC after the separation from NIOC, held 40 percent of the shares. Royal Dutch Shell and Compagnie Française des Pétroles, respectively, took 14 and 6 percent of the shares. The remaining shares were allocated to five American companies. Under this new contract, Iran accepted to share the profit of oil on a 50–50 basis like many other Middle Eastern countries while it would have no influence on consortium management (Mohaddes and Pesaran 2013).

Yet, after the coup, the governing regime began to expand national control over all processes related to the oil industry, especially when NIOC became capable of discovering oil and gas fields such as Alborzand Sarājeh. In addition, new contract terms like the one with the Italian State Oil Company, which proposed a 75/25 contract (Mina 2004), revealed the possibility of more favorable oil agreements. The nationalization of the oil industry in Iran and other Middle Eastern countries restructured international oil markets. These countries acquired further power for managing and unilaterally pricing a globally demanded product (Marcel and Mitchel 2006). This authority was substantially highlighted during the Yom Kippur War, when the Organization of the Petroleum Exporting Countries' (OPEC) members increased the oil price by about 70 percent and reduced the production by about 5 percent in response to the diplomatic and military support of Israel by the United States, which resulted in the 1973 oil crisis (Yergin 1991; Oil&GasJournal 2005).

While daily oil production before nationalization was about 0.6 million barrels a day, from 1960 to 1973 this steadily increased to 6 million. During that time, NIOC experienced major development in its activities. This development was not only a result of substantial increases in oil production that generated high revenues for Iran, but also a result of increases in oil prices. Parviz Mina, the director of NIOC in the 1970s and an oil industry expert, declared that:

The important point is that NIOC was different from its counter-parts in other oil producer countries due to the nature of its work, contract types and specific operations that were conducted in Iran. In other countries, except Venezuela which had nationalized the oil industry, until the later 1975 when the OPEC emerged and became active, major international oil companies controlled oil producing processes; NIOC was the only firm in that period of time that was independently able to explore, extract, and export the oil. Given that, the NIOC was accepted by international oil companies as a credible organization that could play a major role in international markets. For instance, when NIOC attempted to cooperate in downstream operations like refining, distribution and selling the oil, international firms enthusiastically wanted to cooperate rather than compete. On one hand, NIOC had vast oil reserves and pro-duction capacities that ranked it second in oil production after Saudi Arabia; therefore, they found the oil resources of Iran, which were managed by NIOC, crucial for the oil consumers in the world. On the other hand, international oil corporations believed that if NIOC cooperated with them in downstream operations, the possi-bility of competition between NIOC and them would substantially decrease. In addition, NIOC was so advanced in technical affairs that it could easily take part in oil projects, as its experts in nego-tiations with foreigner technicians were considered to be so skillful and experienced. (FIS 2017)

By the mid-1970s, it was clear that the 1954 agreement between Iran and the international consortium did not live up to Iranian wishes about nationalization and the management of its oil industry. Consequently, in 1973, the NIOC issued an ultimatum to the consortium claiming that without agreeing on a contract with new terms, Iran would not extend the 1954 contract beyond 1979 and that, from that point onward, the consortium members would be considered Iran's oil customers (Mina 2004). This ultimatum was mentioned by the Shah in 1973:

We have been negotiating with the consortium about oil for a while; these negotiations are neither over nor resulted in anything . . . when we signed the contract in 1954, probably the best thing we could do at that time, it was declared as one of the terms of the contract that the members of consortium should fulfill the interests of Iran in the best manner. We have enough reasons that according to the 1954 agreement, our interests have not been addressed; we have enough reasons that according to the 1954 agreement, the consortium agreement should not be extended beyond 1979 at all. The governing rights of nations allow them to have complete control over their natural resources . . . No company could claim that it is my own business to determine the amount of oil, for instance, that should be extracted; one should avoid over-extraction of oil wells as it might cause the killing of the oil wells; these things have not been addressed in our country and this is not the fulfillment of our interests. . . . (Shah 2014)

Finally, on July 19, 1973, the consortium members agreed on a new 20-year contract named "Sale and Purchase Agreement" in which they would become "privileged" buyers of Iranian oil while leaving the control and management of the oil sector to the Iranians (Mina 2004). This was probably the last major event for NIOC and Iran's oil industry before the 1979 revolution. Parviz Mina stated that: ". . . our efforts at NIOC began after the nationalization of oil and the 1973 contract led to the implementation of the terms of oil nationalization law; since then, NIOC was changed from a local distributer of petroleum products to a major international company. At that time, Fortune magazine ranked the NIOC among the top 5 oil companies that were active globally" (Behzadi 2016).

NIOC After the 1979 Revolution

In 1979, the Shah's regime was overthrown as a result of an unexpected revolution. The 1979 revolution had an anti-Western and anticolonialist nature. The dominant view was that under the Shah, the United States had become a privileged foreign power whose influence was felt through an increased share in Iranian oil exports and a growing role of American advisors in different fields like the military and government (Fadaee 2012). Moreover, the role of the United States in the coup against Mosaddegh's government was carved in Iranians' minds. Furthermore, the Shah's oil policies were heavily criticized before the revolution. Critics considered the vast production of oil a big waste of resources and a source of corruption. As a result, the Interim Government of Iran, established after the revolution, canceled all oil agreements and contracts with international partners in March 1979 and reduced oil production, which led to the 1979 oil crisis. It is noteworthy that, in the months leading up to the revolution, NIOC employees themselves had attempted to impede oil-extracting operations as a form of cooperation with protesters, leading Ayatollah Khomeini to declared that "the employees of NIOC and the oil industry, in the most crucial situations, have served the revolution and their Islamic home country in the best way; the value of their rivalry with the Shah's regime, refusing of oil extraction for foreigners, and harming foreigners' interests would not be forgotten" (Khomeini 1989).

In 1980, Iraq declared war on Iran and its forces invaded the southern parts of the country where most oil facilities were located. As a result of war hardships and technical difficulties, NIOC's productivity dropped significantly and it took a long time, until 2003, before it could regain the previous production level of 4 million barrels a day (Mohaddes and Pesaran 2013). Despite the above-mentioned obstacles, NIOC never stopped its oil-producing processes during the Iran–Iraq war. As Parviz Mina stated:

> It is wonderful that despite the institutional change as a result of the revolution and the collapse of the previous system, the oil industry of Iran never stopped working; even in its worst conditions. While in the war between Iran and Iraq, the oil constructions and infrastructures were threatened and damaged by the air attacks and missiles, the technical experts were so skillful that they could work under these unusual conditions and keep the oil refining processes moving. This happened because the established infrastructures and the trained human resources were so difficult to destroy. Above all else, the ability to distribute and sell the oil in international markets after the revolution was the outcome of our attempts in attracting customers and establishing connections with global markets; it was those customers who bought the oil after the revolution. In fact, the structures and the management of NIOC was the main reason of its survival and it is not something simple. (FIS 2017)

After the Iran–Iraq war ended in 1988, the country needed construction plans to rebuild itself. Similar to the Shah's state before the 1979 revolution, the Revolutionary State considered oil revenues as crucial for the implementation of its economic and development policy (Sharifi 2009). Therefore, almost all governments after the revolution tried to increase the level of petroleum production (Donya-e-Eqtesad 2014). However, due to the sanctions imposed by the United States after the revolution (Mohaddes and Pesaran 2013), the Iranian petroleum industry faced serious obstacles. In response, the NIOC attempted to fulfill its technological needs through local producers by financing and supporting them (NIOC 2017), leading the NIOC toward adopting a more localized approach.

NIOC Today

In 2011, sanctions were imposed on Iran's oil sector by the United Nations and Western countries in response to Iran's nuclear activities. These sanctions decreased Iran's oil exports by more than a half. While Iran could export about 2.8 million barrels per day in July 2011, its export fell to 1 million barrels in July 2012 (Rahmat 2015). After the sanctions were lifted in 2015, NIOC increased its exports to more than 2 million barrels a day (Iraneconomist 2017). In addition, the Ministry of Petroleum has designed contracts with new terms in order to form new agreements with international oil corporations, which have been detached from the Iranian oil industry for many years. The Ministry of Petroleum, of which NIOC is a subsidiary, has declared that new contracts named Iran Petroleum Contracts (IPC) would boost NIOC's performance and facilitate technology transfer from international companies (NIOC 2017).

However, the new contracts have raised opposition from those who are concerned about the undermining of Iran's control over its national resources. The opponents believe that the new contracts would undermine the authority of NIOC and lead to the confiscation of Iranian oil by international companies (Kayhan 2016). This faction claims that it is unreasonable to delegate the oil-producing processes to international corporations while Iranians themselves have the technical ability to do so (IRIB 2017). Despite the major protest against the IPC, in July 2017 Iran and Total, the French oil and gas company, signed a 20-year cooperation contract with a value of 4.8 billion USD. Nevertheless, NIOC continues its strategy to strengthen its abilities as a means to secure its independency from foreign countries and companies.

Conclusion

Iran's oil industry and NIOC have always been under domestic pressure to maintain control over Iranian oil reserves. Prior to the 1979 revolution, the dominance of a state logic in the sector exerted pressure to nationalize the oil industry. This logic emerged as a counterforce to the market forces that dominated the Iranian oil sector in its early years. It was later consolidated as the dominant logic under the Pahlavi regime due to the need for resources to fund modernization and development programs. This state logic continued to be influential in the sector even after the 1979 revolution, primarily because it resonated with the appointment of Ayatollah Khomeini, who for long had criticized foreign control over Iran's natural resources and who was famous for his anti-American, pro-Islamic, and native-oriented views. Because local ownership and control of the oil industry became a symbol of independence and competence of Iran, NIOC continued to retain control over the management of oil-producing operations.

In conclusion, although NIOC has experienced great ups and downs through its history and has been detached from the community of international oil corporations, it has remained one of the giants of the oil industry in the world, partially as a result of expertise and relations nurtured during earlier eras. For scholars and practitioners interested in globalization, the case of NIOC illustrates that locally emerging alternatives to globalization and liberalization, as seen in Iran, should not necessarily be thought of as incompatible with globalization. Instead, we expect that domestic and local globalization alternatives will emerge and evolve in conjunction with continued globalization. The case of NIOC shows that past experience coupled with a favorable domestic and international network position may allow firms from such contexts to survive and thrive, even as domestic alternatives emerge and other parts of society become subject to antiglobalist sentiments.

References

Abrahamian, E. 2008. *A History of Modern Iran*. New York: Cambridge University Press.

Khomeini, A. 1989. *Message to the Employees of Oil Industry*. January 10. www.imam-khomeini.ir, (accessed July 15, 2017).

Bamberg, J. 1994. *The History of the British Petroleum Company: The Anglo-Iranian Years 1928-1954*. Vol. 2. New York: Cambridge University Press.

Behzadi, S. 2016. *Parviz Mina: The Shah played a first and major role in success of 1973 contract with consortium*. May 07. fa.rfi.fr., (accessed July 10, 2017).

Donya-e-Eqtesad. 2014. *The Performance of Three Previous Goverments about Oil*. March 03. http://donya-e-eqtesad.com/news/789021 (accessed July 10, 2017).

Fadaee, S. 2012. *Social Movements in Iran: Environmentalism and Civil Society*. London: Routledge.

Ferrier, R.W. 1982. *The History of the British Petroleum Company: The Developing Years*. Vol. 1. New York: Cambridge University Press.

FIS. 2017. *The Evolution of the Oil Industry of Iran: a Look from the Inside*. http://fis-iran.org/en/node/3087, (accessed July 10, 2017).

Gasiorowski, M. 1987. "The 1953 Coup D'etat in Iran." *International Journal of Middle East Studies* 19, no. 3, pp. 261–286.

Gasiorowski, M. and M. Byrne. 2004. *Mohammad Mosaddeq and the 1953 Coup in Iran*. New York: Syracuse University Press.

Greenwood, R., A.M. Díaz, S.X. Li, and J.C. Lorente. 2010. "The Multiplicity of Institutional Logics and the Heterogeneity of Organizational Responses." *Organization Science* 2, no. 2, pp. 521–539.

Iraneconomist. 2017. *Zangeneh: the exportation of Iran oil has reached more that 2.6 million barrels a day*. iraneconomist.com (accessed July 10, 2017).

IRIB. 2017. *The Ambiguousness of New Oil Contracts for the Energy Commission of Majlis*. majlestv.ir (accessed July 15, 2017).

Kayhan. 2016. *The New Oil Contracts Fulfill 100 Percent of Foreigners' Interests*. http://kayhan.ir/fa/mobile/news/64813/620 (accessed July 10, 2017).

Keddie, N.R. 1981. *Roots of Revolution: An Interpretive History of Modern Iran*. New Haven: Yale University Press.

Kinzer, S. 2003. *All the Shah's Men: An American Coupand the Roots of Middle East Terror*. New Jersey: John Wiley & Sons.

Marcel, V., and J.V. Mitchel. 2006. *Oil Titans: National Oil Companies in the Middle East*. Baltimore: Brookings Institution Press.

Mina, P. 2004. *Oil Agreements in Iran*. http://www.iranicaonline.org/articles/oil-agreements-in-iran (accessed July 15, 2017).

Mohaddes, K., and M.H. Pesaran. 2013. *One Hundred Years of Oil Income and the Iranian Economy: A Curse or a Blessing?* Working Paper No. 4118, Munich: CESifo.

NIOC. 2017. *Oil through the Development Path.* http://www.nioc.ir (accessed July 10, 2017).

Oil&GasJournal. 2005. *The 1973 Oil Embargo: Its History, Motives, and Consequences.* http://www.ogj.com (Accessed July 10, 2017).

Rahmat, B. 2015. *The Impact of Sanctions on Iran's Oil Exportation.* www.ireconomy.ir (Accessed July 10, 2017).

Shah, M.R. 2014. *MohammadReza Shah's Speech about Oil on 3 Bahman 1351.* https://mashruteh.org (accessed July 15, 2017).

Sharifi, M. 2009. "Iran's Paradox of Oil and Development." *Political and International Research* 1, no. 2, pp. 139–154.

Thornton, P.H, and W. Ocasio. 1999. "Institutional Logics and the Historical Contingency of Power in Organizations: Executive Succession in the Higher Education Publishing Industry, 1958–1990." *American Journal of Sociology* 105, no. 3, pp. 801–843.

Thornton, P.H, W. Ocasio, and M. Lounsbury. 2012. *The Institutional Logics Perspectiv: A New Aproach to Culture, Structure and Process.* Oxford: Oxford University Press.

Yazdani, S. 2017. *The Coups of Iran.* Tehran: Mahi Publication.

Yergin, D. 1991. *The Prize: The Epic Quest for Oil, Money, and Power.* New York: Simon and Schuster.

CHAPTER 7

Local Content Policies

Global versus National?

Irina Heim

Emergence of Economic Nationalism

It is now a widely accepted opinion that those countries that managed to catch up with developed, high-income countries are the ones whose governments proactively promoted domestic structural change, encouraging the search for new business models and markets and channeling resources into promising new activities. Empirical evidence shows this in early Germany, the United States, Japan, Korea, Taiwan, and even China. None of the countries that strictly followed the Washington Consensus demonstrated comparable success in terms of technological upgrade, economic growth, and poverty reduction (Altenburg 2011).

The recent rise of skepticism toward globalization comes from increased inequality and expansion of technological innovations, whereby some blue-collar jobs are increasingly becoming redundant. These trends have expressed itself in the decision of the United Kingdom to leave the European Union (Brexit) and the result of 2016 US presidential election. Concerns in the countries regarding consequences of globalization have led to the fact that the neoliberal order is now being reconfigured, with a greater focus on national interests versus global interests.

Globalization Alternatives and the Multinational Corporations

These changes put pressure on multinational corporations (MNCs) operating globally. Compared to the 1980s when MNCs expanded to transitional economies due to the collapse of planned economics, the 2010s was characterized by increased skepticism toward global expansions. There is also an increased focus on the behavior and strategies of MNCs in these new conditions. These issues are being addressed by governments, as well as international organizations. MNCs often raise concern that local content policies (LCPs), particularly in the oil and gas sectors, lead to increased costs. However, taking into consideration that most international oil and gas companies (IOCs), operating in developing countries such as Kazakhstan, represent home countries where natural resources are already exhausted or they do not own the resources (e.g., ENI—Italy, Total—France, Royal Dutch Shell—the United Kingdom and the Netherlands, INPEX—Japan, or CNPC—China), IOCs should take into consideration concerns of the citizens of these developing countries on the sovereignty of their natural resources. For example, the Constitution of the Republic of Kazakhstan states that its natural resources belong to its citizens. Therefore, the citizens would like to have control over how these resources are used and how the wealth from its sale is distributed. This agenda pushes the governments of developing countries to enact industrial policies stimulating domestic development.

This chapter focuses on the current challenges IOCs from developed countries face while participating in oil exploratory projects in developing nations, which types of strategies work best, and how activities should be organized. Additionally, it examines what responses governments take and the implications of these strategies for MNCs. Research on these issues aims to generate new insights into the relationship between firm-level decision-making by MNCs, in relation to governments, and the increasingly antiglobal environment they operate in. In particular, the research addresses the issue of LCPs in the oil and gas industry, a type of performance requirement in resource-rich developing countries.

Local Content Policies in Resource-Rich Countries

Local content is an oil sector governance and sustainability policy that aims to encourage participation of domestic companies and redistribute wealth between global value chain suppliers and local companies. It stimulates economic development in resource-rich countries and provides a basis for economic diversification in these countries.

Industrial policy can be defined as strategic efforts of a government to encourage structural changes and development leading to competitiveness via growth in manufacturing and related services sector (Aiginger 2007; Altenburg, 2011). Traditional industrial policies of different types include tariffs (import substitution policy), subsidies (special economic zones), and local content requirements (local industry development). In contrast to traditional industrial policies such as import substitution that were heavily criticized, LCPs in the oil and gas sector have been adopted by different developing countries such as Brazil, Kazakhstan, Kuwait, Nigeria, Indonesia, Uganda, Tanzania, and many others.

Definitions of a "LCP" may vary depending on the context and user. From the foreign direct investment (FDI) perspective, LCP can be defined as "a policy governing foreign investors or investments that aims to actively embed foreign investment in, and catalyze spillovers into and linkages with, the domestic economy. This definition includes, but is not limited to, measures expressly requiring or incentivizing use of local goods, services, and labor. It can also include measures such as those requiring foreign investors to incorporate firms in the host economy or to make intra-firm expenditures in the host economy" (Johnson 2016).

LCPs have emerged over the past decades in resource-rich countries as a result of competition between the main stakeholders such as oil and gas global and local companies, countries, governments, citizens, and communities for the wealth created by the energy sector. It also became popular in certain industries such as automotive, renewable energy, electronic, and pharmaceutical. It was used as a development model that protected these sectors from international competition in the early stage of industrialization.

An initial economic explanation as to why protection schemes are necessary in the oil and gas sector focused on the phenomena of "Dutch disease" or disproportions in the country's economic development reflected in a decline in the manufacturing and agriculture sectors while leading to a boom in the natural resource sector (Corden 1984) and "recourse course" expressed in the inability of countries rich in natural resources to use wealth to develop their economies leading to low economic growth (Sachs and Warner 1995). Although many countries, including developed ones, have adopted LCPs at some time in their history, it was later significantly constrained by supranational organizations such as the World Trade Organization (WTO) as one of the forms of performance requirements prohibited by WTO. Kazakhstan's accession to the WTO in 2016 raised the following question: how can the Government of Kazakhstan adjust its local development policies to the WTO requirements which prohibit performance measurements in order to enhance cooperation between international and local oil and gas companies and grow the economy?

Case Study: Karachaganak Petroleum Operating Consortium and Local Content Policies in Kazakhstan

This case study[1] was conducted in order to examine the responses of IOCs operating in Kazakhstan on local content practices applied by the government, the National Agency for Local Content Development, National Welfare Fund "Samruk-Kazyna," and the National Oil and Gas Company (NOC) "KazMunayGas." The case is interesting given the large volumes of natural resources and geopolitical importance of Kazakhstan. Since its independence in 1991, the country attracted significant foreign direct investments (Delevic and Heim 2017), with most investments in the natural resource sector. Local content requirements in the oil and gas sector include those for local content in goods, works and services, and personnel, as well as participation in social initiatives.

Kazakhstan has three major oilfield exploratory projects: Karachaganak Petroleum Operations (KPO), Tengizchevroil (TCO), and North Caspian Operating Company (NCOC). One of them—the Karachaganak oilfield—is located near Uralsk, a town in West Kazakhstan oblast (WKO) in the northwest of Kazakhstan. The field has one of the world's largest hydrocarbon reserves. It has about 1.2 billion barrels of oil and

---

[1] The case study is based on the film produced by Karachaganak Petroleum Operations and available at YouTube.

gas condensate and 1.35 trillion cubic meters of gas. The field is of paramount importance to the economy of the region and the country. It provides half of the gas produced in Kazakhstan and about 15 percent of liquid hydrocarbons. The international consortium responsible for its development and operation is KPO which includes IOCs Royal Dutch Schell, ENI, Chevron, Lukoil, and NOC KazMunayGas.

KPO General Director Renato Maroli explained that the company is applying modern technology in the development of the Karachaganak field, one of the most complex reservoirs from a geological standpoint. The goal is to provide stable revenue for Kazakhstan and achieve sustainable development. The Karachaganak partners fully supported the Republic of Kazakhstan's plans and initiatives aimed toward local content development and industrialization. A noteworthy initiative includes the Kazakhstan 2050 Strategy and Industrial Innovative Programme ("New Industrialisation"). The parent company invested nearly US $22 billion in the exploration of this field. The government of Kazakhstan preferred that financial resources were spent in the country and not overseas. With this aim the LCP was introduced.

In order to meet these institutional requirements, KPO takes an active part in the development of local content through the implementation of the Aktau Declaration (Aktau Declaration, 2012). This is a memorandum of understanding pertaining to the development of the domestic industry. It was signed by the operators of three major exploratory projects in Kazakhstan: NCOC, TCO, KPO, and NOC KazMunayGas. In addition, KPO also cooperated with the local authority ("Akimat") and took on a number of other activities.

According to Altai Kulginov (KPO 2017), head of WKO (akim):

International companies as Karachaganak consortium open huge opportunities to our local companies. [Through the cooperation with international companies and adoption of higher quality standards], local companies cooperating with KPO project can improve their standards, the quality of producing goods and services. Karachaganak project invested in social infrastructure projects of the region more than $300 million. This is support for improving of our infrastructure and also life quality of our population.

According to KPO, they made local industry development an integral part of their strategy. The company contributed in the development of local suppliers, goods, and services and implemented several projects in support of national manufacturing. The project focused on the cooperation between the international and local manufacturers and enabled them to integrate and transfer their advanced technologies to the industrial sector of Kazakhstan.

According to KPO Vice General Director Marat Karimov (KPO 2017),

We maintain local content database, where more than 3,800 companies are registered. For the first half of 2016 the local content in our company reached about 49 percent or $280 million. Since the start of production sharing agreement, we paid about $5.7 billion to local companies.

The company believes that the implementation of large oil and gas projects such as Karachaganak had an impact on the development of the national economy. It created an environment where local companies could achieve competitiveness through the application of best practices from the world's leading firms. The new knowledge gained was transferred to the oil and gas industry and spilled over into other industries. The KPO consortium signed several joint agreements geared toward the development of production and service clusters for Karachaganak and other oil and gas projects in Kazakhstan. Examples of successful development of partnerships included cooperation with Aksai industrial park, Tenaris, and GE Oil & Gas (KPO, 2014). In order to perform design and engineering work on complex production facilities, KPO established partnerships with major international engineering companies such as Tecnomare (ENI group) and the Kazakh company Caspian Engineering. Partnerships were also established with Worley Parsons and the KGNT Kazgiproneftetrans engineering company, a local Kazakh company. These joint ventures dealt with engineering and design for key projects, such as the KPC gas debottlenecking project. Extensive operational cooperation facilitated the transfer of international best practices to the Kazakh partners. The cooperation agreement strengthened the capacity of local suppliers, created new jobs, and stimulated the development of the industrial sector of the region.

Beibit Sabirov (KPO 2017), KPO local business development controller, explained that:

> KPO is making great efforts to promote development of partnership between foreign and local service companies and equipment manufacturers. Also KPO signed a number of joint agreement in development of production and services clusters in the Republic of Kazakhstan . . . The result of this work includes signing an agreement on technical cooperation between the world's leading manufacturer of power equipment ABB and Ural Electric LLP which aims at aligning the manufacturer of the electricity distribution and control equipment with the cutting-edge technology of ABB company. The total value of investment will amount 1.5 billion Tenge and implies creation of 150 jobs in Uralsk city.

In 2016, KPO took an active part in implementing a number of initiatives to increase local content. Together with other major IOCs as well as local and foreign engineering companies, the management of KPO met with representatives of various regions of Kazakhstan. During these meetings the IOCs had a chance to present their requirements relating to goods, services, and technology. The KPO management visited industrial companies in Karaganda, North Kazakhstan, Atyrau oblast and signed a number of joint agreements aimed at local content development. A memorandum of understanding was signed between KPO and a British company William Hare Limited (SGT Group, 2017), which aimed to elevate work processes in Kazakhstan's manufacturing and steel industries. In June 2016, KPO representatives visited the facilities of the largest companies in the region and provided information on the company's procedures, registration, and vendor's database, as well as the process of prequalification and tender requirements.

According to Bakytzhan Doskaziyev (KPO 2017), KPO local content development manager:

> In February 2016 . . . the participants of Aktau Declaration launched a single database of suppliers ALASH which will become a single window for Kazakhstani suppliers to the procurement process. . . .

In May 2016, KPO held an informational workshop on a KPC gas debottlenecking project for the representatives of Kazakh companies. The main objective was to provide domestic manufacturers and service providers the opportunity to participate in the project through the establishment of joint ventures. The event was attended by representatives of the more than 40 local enterprises, state authorized bodies, and specialized associations, such as "National Agency for Development of Local Content," and the Union of service companies of Kazakhstan. The First Innovation forum of WKO "Akzhaiyk Invest 2016" was held in July 2016 in the new KPO office in Uralsk city. It was organized by Ural, WKO akimat, a social enterprise company and KPO. The forum was attended by the representatives of WKO and a number of national companies and associations, the national Chamber of Entrepreneurs of Kazakhstan, Kazakhstan Union of oilfield companies "Kazservice," Entrepreneur development Fund "DAMU" as well as small and medium-sized companies in the region. KPO and Karachaganak partners aimed to strengthen local capacity. The goal was achieved through the implementation of sustainable development programs and the transfer of innovative technologies and skills.

The company stated that the objectives of the KPO local content program coincided with the development and growth initiatives of the domestic industry and local oil and gas projects such as Karachaganak. KPO implemented several projects that developed manufacturing capabilities not only in the West Kazakhstan region but also in other regions of Kazakhstan. For example, KPO built threading facilities with a capacity of 45,000 tons per year in the city of Aktau. Additionally, KPO signed a contract with the international manufacturing company Tenaris Global Services for the provision of casing and tubing goods.

According to Samat Kulchikov (KPO 2017), sales manager of Tenaris Global Services (Kazakhstan),

> Our plant is located in specialized economic zone of Aktau city . . . This is the contribution of Tenaris company into development of local content and creation of new jobs in Kazakhstan. We are happy, we have been able to implement this project with support of KPO.

KPO reported that they implemented several large-scale projects to develop social infrastructure in the WKO. Every year a budget of $20 million is provided for the purpose. Additionally, from 2014 to 2016, over $10 million was budgeted each year for the implementation of similar projects in WKO. From 1998 to the present, the volume of KPO investments in social infrastructure development projects has exceeded $300 million. Karachaganak investments had a positive effect on the social reconstruction of West Kazakhstan. The priorities for social infrastructure projects are determined by the WTO akimat. This program included construction of health, education, culture, and sport facilities. These projects were implemented with the participation of local Kazakh contractors. The constant attention to the KPO activities paid by the Republic of Kazakhstan Ministry of Energy and the authority under cooperation with WKO leadership contributed to a significant improvement in the implementation of the projects as well as the overall socioeconomic situation in the region.

Concluding Thoughts

Kazakhstan had supported and developed local content in the oil and gas industry since the declaration of its independence in the 1990s. In the new millennium, the government pursued local content development of the Kazakhstani economy through primary and secondary measures such as laws, decrees, and quotas created by the legislative and executive branches of government. The IOCs in Kazakhstan used different approaches to assess local content and relied on various documents such as production-sharing agreements, as well as local and international contracts. With introduction of the Law of the Republic of Kazakhstan "On subsoil and subsoil use" (New Subsoil Use Law) in 2010, LCPs in Kazakhstan included procurement, labor, and technology transfer policies and social projects. The country's recent accession to the WTO in 2016 limited the use of LCPs, as WTO prohibits performance requirements, that is, "stipulations, imposed on investors, requiring them to meet certain specified goals with respect to their operations in the host country" (UNCTAD 2003, p. 2). However, Kazakhstan managed to negotiate a 5-year transition period for subsoil use contracts signed before January 1, 2015.

Requirements in contracts regarding the local content in goods would take effect only until January 1, 2021. Newly concluded subsoil use contracts shall not contain any requirements related to local content in goods or preferential treatment to Kazakhstani producers in competitive bids (e.g., the existing requirement for Kazakh bids to be favored if they are within 20 percent of the foreign bids).

Some local content requirements in work and services as well as in personnel remain in effect. For example, the minimum local content of works and services in the newly concluded subsoil use contracts states that existing subsoil use contracts signed from September 2011 to the date of Kazakhstan's accession to the WTO must be decreased to 50 percent. In addition, Kazakhstani producers of works and services must be granted a 20 percent reduction in the price of their bids during the tender procedure. However, Kazakhstani producers are expected to meet the requirements of Kazakhstan law on all technical regulations.

IOCs when developing projects in resource-rich countries should take a strategic approach to local content policies and recognize wider business benefits of sharing wealth and creating value from oil and gas beyond the payment of royalties and taxes. IOCs can demonstrate commitment to the host country's LCPs through different documents such as internal LCPs, sustainability reports, and memorandums signed with other oil and gas consortiums and local authorities. The strategic approach should focus on cooperation with local companies, enabling integration with the global value chain and the transfer of knowledge and technologies through partnership with local and foreign companies. Maintaining a local supplier's database and conducting "informational workshops" with the aim to advice local companies on business opportunities would be helpful. Participating in joint agreements on development of local production and service cluster may lead to the enhancement of local capabilities. Cooperation with international service and manufacturing companies who are interested to set up their greenfield operations may therefore lead to the inflow of FDI in the host countries. These operations can be located in special economic zones.

In conclusion, globalization is increasing economic interdependence of national economies across the world through increases in international trade, capital and technology flows, and migration (Joshi 2009). LCP aims to substitute import and increase a share of local labor force and therefore is considered as a manifestation of economic nationalism and a process of deglobalization, that is, diminishing integration between nation states. Although there are some challenges associated with the development of local industry in Kazakhstan and local capacity remains low (Kalyuzhnova et al. 2016), recent research demonstrates that LCPs have positive effect on the local economy, have links with firm competitiveness and decision on export, and foster firm competitiveness under certain conditions (Azhgaliyeva et al. 2016). Citizens of resource-rich countries require their government to regulate oil and gas industries. As a result, growth of economic nationalism in these countries may be observed. International companies when doing business under such conditions should take into consideration that strategic localization and harmonious relationships with stakeholders can lead to international project success.

References

Aiginger, K. 2007. "Industrial Policy: A Dying Breed or a Re-emerging Phoenix". *Journal of Industry Competition and Trade* 7, pp. 297–323.

Aktau Declaration. 2012. "Aktau Declaration on Joint Actions - Expression of Support." https://www.aktaudeclaration.org/index.php?option=com_conten t&view=article&id=96&Itemid=869&lang=en. (accessed May 22, 2017).

Altenburg, T. 2011. "Industrial Policy in Developing Countries: Overview and Lessons from Seven Country Cases" Bonn: DIE (Discussion Paper 4/2011).

Azhgaliyeva, D., M. Belitski, and Y. Kalyuzhnova. 2016. "Local Content Policy and Sustainable Firm Performance: Case Study Kazakhstan". Unpublished paper.

Corden, W.M. 1984. "Booming Sector and Dutch Disease Economics: Survey and Consolidation". *Oxford Economic Papers* 36, pp. 359–380.

Delevic, U., and I. Heim. 2017. "Institutions in Transition: Is the EU Integration Process Relevant for Inward FDI in Transition European Economies?" *Eurasian Journal of Economics and Finance* 5, no. 1, pp. 16–32, doi: 10.15604/ ejef.2017.05.01.002

"Foreign Direct Investment and Performance Requirements: New Evidence from Selected Countries". United Nations Conference on Trade and Development (UNCTAD) 2003. http://unctad.org/en/docs/ iteiia20037_en.pdf (accessed May 22, 2017).

Johnson, L. 2016. *Space for Local Content Policies and Strategies*. Bonn: Deutsche Gesellschaft für Internationale Zusammenarbeit.

Joshi, R.M. 2009. *International Business*. New Delhi and New York: Oxford University Press.

Kalyuzhnova, Y., Nygaard, C., Omarov, Y., and Saparbayev, A., 2016. *Local content policies in resource-rich countries*. New York, NY: Palgrave Macmillan. https://doi.org/10.1057/978-1-137-44786-9

KPO. 2014. "Karachaganak Sustainability Report, 2014." http://www.raexpert.kz/docs/annual_contest/kpo/SR_KPO_2014_en.pdf (accessed May 22, 2017).

KPO. 2017. "Partnership for the Benefit of Industrial Potential Development of Kazakhstan." https://www.youtube.com/watch?v=NDwWSECxMtw (accessed May 22, 2017).

Sachs, J., and A.M. Warner. 1995. "Natural Resources Abundance and Economic Growth". *NBER working paper series*. *Working paper 5398*. Cambridge: National Bureau of Economic Research.

SGT Group. 2017. *Effective Cooperation*. http://www.anm.kz/en/contacts/107-29071 (accessed May 22, 2017).

SECTION 4

Businesses and Industries

CHAPTER 8

Unglobal Finance

Informal and Alternative Banking Activities

Les Dlabay

While globalization is at the forefront of international business, vast numbers of people work and conduct transactions removed from registered companies. In these informal economic settings, financial activities often occur through nonconventional channels that include:

Amaka stores cash in a wall of her hut, or buries banknotes in the ground. These actions hide money from family and friends who might demand financial assistance.

At a *tanda* meeting in a Mexico City, Gracia deposits 50 pesos. This week is her turn to receive the payout of 600 pesos to buy a used oven for her home-based bakery business.

In the Laguna province market, in the Philippines, Romeo needs to borrow 1,500 pesos for his inventory. While a 2-day loan has an annualized interest rate of 1,000 percent, Romeo's annualized return will be 1,600 percent.

Facing the prospect of unexpected medical expenses, Askhat contributes an additional amount each week to the insurance fund of his savings group.

Over two billion people conduct business using informal financial services outside of the formal banking system (Singh 2013). With a limited financial infrastructure in many countries, along with a strong cultural tradition, these "off the books" monetary activities facilitate transactions for underserved populations (Adams and Fitchett 1992).

Providers of alternative banking activities serve three groups of clients: (1) *unbanked,* those without access to formal financial services; (2) *debanked,* people who previously used formal financial services but no longer do so; and (3) *underbanked,* formal financial services customers who also use informal banking.

Informal Economic Activities

In every economic setting, some business occurs beyond the purview of registered enterprises. Estimates of informal economic activities range from 10 to 20 percent in industrialized nations to over 60 percent in developing economies. These business activities are known by a variety of terms (Exhibit 8.1), which vary based on the nature of the transaction, culture, and the political environment.

Exhibit 8.1
Informal Economic Activity Descriptors

informal economy	cash economy	hidden economy
shadow economy	parallel economy	unofficial economy
dual economy	illicit economy	unrecorded economy
underground economy	unobserved economy	black market
invisible economy	street economy	ghetto economy
economy of affection	twilight economy	subsistence economy
second economy	alternative economy	supplementary economy
unreported economy	unregistered economy	unregulated economy
off the books	subterranean economy	unstructured economy
under the table	temporary economy	transitory economy
underside economy	underneath economy	survival employment
unauthorized enterprises	stealth business	clandestine economy
secret economy	undercover economy	covert economy
sharing economy	underbelly economy	concealed economy
gray market	casual work	family-enterprise sector
home-based economy	unseen economy	subversive economy

irregular economy	transient economy	bazaar economy
economy of the people	unorganized economy	on-demand economy
unplanned economy	nonformal economy	illegal economy
intermediate economy	commodity economy	one-person enterprise
evasive economy	elusive economy	peer-to-peer economy
extralegal economy	nonofficial economy	precarious economy

Informal economic activities involve business ranging from street selling and home-based manufacturing to distributing stolen merchandise and operating unregistered taxi services. An often overlooked element in this shadow economy is financial services.

Alternative Financial Services

Even when operating with an extralegal status, entrepreneurs and workers require borrowing and other financial activities. Bruton et al. (2012) note the need for trust in a setting that involves extending and repaying a non-legally binding loan. While credit is the main informal financial service, a range of others exist. Collins et al. (2009) emphasize that saving activities often surpass borrowing transactions.

Preference for informal financial services often exists despite high borrowing costs and inconsistent quality. Collins et al. (2009), studying participants in Bangladesh, India, and South Africa, report varied incentives for using informal financial services. These include flexible loan terms from family and friends, and reduced travel time. Alternative banking customers note greater security when borrowing from a moneylender— a person they know and see regularly. The individuals and institutions that are financial service providers (Exhibit 8.2) may be viewed in three categories:

1. *Formal* financial service providers, such as banks and credit unions, meet all financial regulatory requirements in a country.
2. *Semiformal* providers have a legal business status but are not subject to the nation's regulations for financial institutions.
3. *Informal* providers, both individual and group-based, involve unregistered enterprises.

Exhibit 8.2

Financial Service Providers

Formal

- Banks
- Mutual savings banks
- Savings and loan associations
- Credit unions

Semiformal

- Credit cooperatives
- Nongovernmental organizations (NGOs)
- Pawnshops
- Microfinance institutions (MFIs)
- Postal service
- Mobile phone banking networks

Informal

Individual providers

- Family, friends
- Moneyguards, deposit collectors
- Moneylenders
- Informal currency traders
- Shop owners, loan sharks

Group-based providers

- Self-help groups (SHGs)
- Village savings and loan associations (VSLAs)
- Rotating savings and credit associations (RoSCAs)
- Remittance networks
- Accumulating savings and credit associations (ASCAs)
- Microinsurance

Most individual providers do business with a few customers; group-based and semiformal providers interact with a large number of clients. *Social collateral* is crucial for informal financial services involving a trust-based relationship. Personal knowledge of a potential borrower along with guidance from trusted clients is used to determine credit merit (Dlabay 2015). The focus of this discussion involves the semiformal and informal segments.

Semiformal Financial Services

Beyond formal financial services, various organizations serve underbanked and unbanked consumers. These institutions, while not subject to formal financial regulations, operate under the auspices of general and commercial laws.

Credit Cooperatives. Serving financial needs in a community, credit cooperatives offer loans, and sometimes savings accounts, to their member-owners. These community-based, nonprofit microfinance institutions (MFIs) are often organized with a *village banking model* in a limited geographic area. The cooperative financial services model is used in many areas of Asia, including savings and credit cooperatives and the Small Farmers Cooperatives Limited in Nepal (Mercy Corps 2008); State Cooperative Banks, District Central Cooperative Banks, Primary Agricultural Credit Societies, and Primary Cooperative Agriculture and Rural Development Banks in India; and rural cooperatives in China with a "quasi legality" status (Tsai 2004).

Pawnshops. Charging exorbitant rates on loans, pawnbrokers negotiate a high volume of short-term small loans secured by a physical asset such as gold, jewelry, or desirable consumer goods. Pawnbrokers often operate a retail store to sell goods that are not redeemed (Ledgerwood 2013). Many countries have regulations and require registration of pawnshops.

Postal Service. In Asian and African countries, many previously ruled by Britain, post offices offer financial services. Operating as "India Post," with more than 150,000 offices, this government-operated entity provides unbanked people with savings accounts, money transfers, money orders, life insurance, and mutual funds. Financial services offered through the postal service are common in Côte d'Ivoire, Kenya, Malawi, Pakistan, Namibia, Nigeria, Senegal, Tanzania, Uganda, Vietnam Zimbabwe, and elsewhere.

Nongovernmental Organizations and Microfinance Institutions. Relief and development organizations commonly facilitate activities to provide financial services in informal economic settings. Nongovernmental organizations (NGOs) and MFIs operate locally as well as globally (through a physical or an online presence), and are sometimes referred to as financial intermediary nongovernmental organizations. These MFIs are usually licensed to offer limited financial services such as savings plans and loans (Mercy Corps 2008).

Mobile Phone Banking Networks. *Open banking* involves financial services occurring through a third party, rather than with a formal institution, using apps. The most common of these involves mobile phone banking. In Kenya and other areas of Africa, M-PESA has created a network for payments, loans, money transfers, and remittances. This mobile money system provides financial services for informal business owners, low-income households, rural clients, and others not previously able to access banks, cash machines, and credit cards (Mas and Radcliffe 2010). *Fintech* activities, involving technology-enabled banking and financial services, continue to evolve with apps for budgeting, saving, credit reporting, financial advice, and flexible loan repayment (Financial Solutions Lab).

Individually-Provided Financial Services

Providing loans and storing money with family and friends is the foundation of individual-based informal finance services. In addition, informal financial entrepreneurs meet the demand for borrowing, saving, and other financial services.

Moneylenders. For centuries, individuals have made loans for personal and business needs. Normally using personal funds, moneylenders provide small loans. Most loans are unsecured, involving a personal connection or recommendation of others. At other times, gold, jewelry, or land may serve as collateral. In India, moneylenders may be referred to as *shroffs, seths, sahukars, mahajans,* and *chettis* (Srinivas).

In the Philippines, *5–6 moneylenders* operate in market areas. When obtaining five pesos for a week or just a day, the borrower pays back six, resulting in a 20 percent interest rate for the designated time period. This activity can result in an annual interest rate exceeding 1,000 percent. Most 5–6 borrowings involve short-term loans, with funds used to bridge the time between current expenses and future business revenue (Kondo 2003).

In Indonesian fishing communities, traders lend fishermen. These moneylenders charge no interest. Instead, the traders buy some fish from the borrower below the market price. This agreement allows the trader to profit when the fish are sold; the profit serves as a finance charge for the loan. Fisherman repay the loan from the funds received for the fish they sell (Mohammad and Yunaningsih 2014).

Shop Owners and Loan Sharks. Shoppers often receive credit from retailers, allowing customers to buy on account. Amounts owed are usually repaid within a few days or at the end of the month. In West Java, *warungs* are family-owned stores selling diesel fuel to fishermen. Customers are charged prices 10 to 15 percent higher for items purchased on account, and are allowed to repay when funds are available from the sale of their fish catch (Mohammad and Yunaningsih 2014).

Common throughout the world are *loan sharks*, charging exorbitant interest rates. These black market lenders in China are known to charge interest rates as much as 70 percent (Barboza 2011). In many low-income communities, loan sharks may seize personal property when payments are late.

Deposit Collectors. In many cultures, people receive frequent requests for money from family and friends. To circumvent these requests for financial assistance, storing cash elsewhere is necessary. Without access to a formal financial institution, people make use of *deposit collectors*, or *moneyguards,* a tradition among indigenous savers. The fee for this service can be as high as 10 percent of the amount saved.

Susu collectors in Ghana serve marketplace traders providing a valuable service to clients since few formal financial institutions offer low-balance savings accounts. Collins et al. (2009) report that moneyguarding was common among households in Bangladesh, India, and South Africa. Using a deposit collector is not without risk since funds may not be available when needed, or a collector may depart a community (Ledgerwood 2013).

Informal Currency Traders. Foreign exchange often occurs through a retail enterprise that may serve as a "front" for unregistered money exchange activities. Based on responses from U.S. embassy representatives, Dlabay and Reger (2007) observed that countries with lower economic development experienced a higher incidence of informal foreign exchange activities. A parallel currency exchange market that included acceptance of an adjoining nation's currency was especially prevalent in southern Africa.

Group-Based Financial Services

Locally formed and self-managed financial service groups are referred to as "informal credit markets" (Ghate 1992). These community-based assemblies are formed based on local cultural norms and business practices to provide financial services within a village or region.

Self-Help Groups. In certain areas of South Asia and Southeast Asia, especially India, *self-help groups* (SHGs) are village assemblies, usually in rural areas, that come together to form an informal savings and credit organization. Usually involving 15 to 20 women, SHGs may also be referred to as savings and credit groups or self-reliant groups (SRGs). The group members are committed to financial and business development activities that benefit all involved (US AID 2008). With a focus on facilitating entrepreneurial activities, SHGs are also a source of social and economic empowerment for women.

Rotating Savings and Credit Associations. Operating in more than 70 countries, rotating savings and credit associations (RoSCAs) are a community-based informal finance service tradition. Ardener and Burman (1996) describe the RoSCA as "an association formed upon a core of participants who make regular contributions to a fund which is given in whole or in part to each contributor in turn." At each RoSCA meeting, funds are collected from each member and distributed to one person. With this arrangement, people otherwise unable to save or obtain credit obtain funds for medical bills or to pay expenses for a family business. RoSCAs operate under names that include *arisans* (Indonesia), *chit funds* (India), *ekub* (Ethiopia), *osusu* (Nigeria), *tandas* (Mexico), and *tontines* (in several Asian and African countries) (Bouman 1995).

RoSCAs also exist in ethnic enclaves of urban areas of industrialized economies. In Los Angeles, people of Korean descent participate in *kyes*. Somali women in the United Kingdom created RoSCAs (Ardener and Burman 1996). In the United States, tandas, also called *cudinas,* may be observed in Latino and Chicano communities (Thompson 2014).

Accumulating Savings and Credit Associations. Expanding on the borrowing activities of RoSCAs, accumulating savings and credit associations (ASCAs) have a savings element. At each meeting, group members deposit an amount. These funds are used to give loans to group members with earnings from interest distributed to group members. One of the major differences of ASCA with RoSCAs is that ASCA funds are not paid out unless loans are requested (Rutherford and Arora 2009).

Village Savings and Loan Associations. Organized with a more prescribed approach than ASCAs, village savings and loan associations (VSLAs) provide members with a safe place to save, borrow, and obtain emergency funds. Using a time-bound model (usually 9 or 12 months), group members deposit funds and, as needed, request loans from the financial pool. At the end of the time period is the *share out*, when saved amounts go back to the VSLA members. In addition, group members receive earnings from the interest earned on loans. This amount is based on a proportion of the amount saved by each participant in the VSLA. After the share out, the group may continue to operate with current or additional members, starting a new cycle.

Strong transparency and member accountability in VSLAs result from an independent and self-managing environment. All financial transactions (savings deposits, loan requests, and repayments) are witnessed by members at the group meeting. Although usually excused from government regulations, VSLAs in some nations may be required to register with a local agency.

Microfinance and development organizations often facilitate the creation of VSLAs to provide low-income clients with access to low-cost loans and savings programs; these include the Aga Khan Foundation, Catholic Relief Services, Freedom from Hunger, Oxfam, World Vision, and World Relief. Some VSLA programs combine financial service activities with income-generating activities. These business development ventures may involve distribution and sales of solar lanterns or other products to address community needs. In other settings, microenterprises may be developed to enhance the availability of seeds, fertilizer, and other agricultural inputs (Rippey and Fowler 2011).

Remittance Networks. Informal money transfer activities operate under names such as *hundi in* South Asia, *feichien* in China, *hui kuan* in Hong Kong, *padala* in the Philippines, and *pheikwan* in Thailand. Many of these networks, especially those in African mineral exporting nations, developed to finance trade and transfer funds against the movement of goods (Isern et al. 2005). Common in the Middle East and Asia, *hawalas* are informal remittance networks used by migrant workers to send funds back to their home countries.

Microinsurance. Financial loss due from risks associated with death, illness, agricultural calamity, and other hazards can be devastating to those operating in the informal economy. Informal insurance programs have surfaced for specific financial needs. Created to cover funeral costs, *burial societies* involve a community-managed savings fund in which participants contribute weekly or monthly payments. A burial society may lend out excess money to earn an additional amount for the fund. Most common in rural areas, *stretcher clubs* exist to address the financial burden of medical emergencies; the plan is named for the traditional transport mode used to carry patients. Payments to the fund are used to cover the costs of health care transportation and medical treatments.

Informal microinsurance programs may also supplement the activities of a savings group or other financial service provider. Contributions of VSLA participants over their savings deposits, for example, may be used for financial emergencies encountered by a group member.

Microfinance organizations, such as ACCION and Opportunity International, have ventured into microinsurance activities. Efforts exist to determine the feasibility and costs for expanding financial service delivery channels to create partnerships for microinsurance programs with MFIs and through mobile phone networks.

Implications for Action

Informal financial services provide capital and cash flow for billions of people. While the ongoing operations of this parallel financial system are vital for people in diverse economic segments, several issues might be considered for continuation of vibrant global business activities.

1. Without regulations, the potential exists for fraud and exploitation by loan sharks, moneylenders, and moneyguards, creating a need to minimize personal and social costs associated with these would-be unethical activities.

2. Formal–informal linkages can create greater business opportunities, as advocated by McGahan (2012). These alliances have the potential of creating *shared value* among the underserved and underrepresented populations (Porter and Kramer 2011).

3. *Financial inclusion* initiatives address concerns associated with exclusion from adequate banking services. Research, policy development, and advocacy are the focus of the Center for Financial Inclusion (www.centerforfinancialinclusion.org) and the Consultative Group to Assist the Poor (www.cgap.org). Of special note in working with underserved populations is My Oral Village (www.myoralvillage .org), which designs financial tools and solutions for individuals lacking the literacy skills to understand written financial records.

4. Financial literacy programs prepare business clients and others for successful use of financial services. These initiatives should involve a joint effort among business, government, and NGOs.

Concluding Comment

People who live, work, and do business in the informal economy frequently lack access to financial services. The gap that exists for underbanked and unbanked consumers is filled by an array of informal and alternative financial products. These unregistered banking activities provide a financial infrastructure for households and entrepreneurs that result in business creation, employment opportunities, community development, and improved quality of life.

References

Adams, D.W., and D.A. Fitchett. (eds.). 1992. *Informal Finance in Low-income Countries*. Boulder: Westview Press.

Ardener, S., and S. Burman. (eds.). 1996. *Money-go-rounds: The Importance of ROSCAs for Women*. Oxford: Berg Publishers.

Barboza, D. 2011. "In Cooling China, Loan Sharks Come Knocking." *The New York Times*, October 13.

Bouman, F. 1995. "ROSCA: On the Origin of the Species." *Savings and Development* XIX, no. 2, p. 129.

Bruton, G.D., R.D. Ireland, and D.K. Ketchen Jr. 2012. "Toward a Research Agenda on the Informal Economy." *Academy of Management Perspectives* 26 no. 3, pp. 1–11.

Collins, D., J. Morduch, S. Rutherford, and O. Ruthven. 2009. *Portfolios of the Poor: How the World's Poor Live on $2 a Day*. Princeton: Princeton University Press.

Dlabay, L. 2015. "Informal Financial Services: A Proposed Research Agenda." In P. Godfrey (ed.) *Management, Society, and the Informal Economy*. New York: Routledge.

Dlabay, L.R., and G. Reger. 2007. "A Regional Comparison of Informal Foreign Exchange Activities: A Qualitative Analysis." Paper presented at the annual meeting of the Midwest Chapter, Academy of International Business, Chicago.

Financial Solutions Lab. n.d. "Meet Nine Innovative Companies Helping Americans Achieve Financial Health." https://www.jpmorganchase.com /corporate/Corporate-Responsibility/document/fincap_cfsi_082016.pdf (accessed November 4, 2017).

Ghate, P. 1992. *Informal Finance: Some Findings from Asia*. Oxford: Asian Development Bank Press, Oxford University Press.

Isern, J., R. Deshpande, and J. Van Doorn. 2005. *Crafting a Money Transfers Strategy: Guidance for Pro-poor Financial Service Providers*. Washington: CGAP.

Kondo, M. 2003. "The Bombay 5-6: Last Resource Informal Financiers for Philippine Micro-enterprises." *Kyoto Review of Southeast Asia*. http:// kyotoreview.org/issue-4/the-bombay-5-6-last-resource-informal-financiers-for-philippine-micro-enterprises/ (accessed November 4, 2017).

Ledgerwood, J. (ed.). 2013. *The New Microfinance Handbook: A Financial Market System Perspective*. Washington: The World Bank.

McGahan, A. 2012. "Challenges of the Informal Economy for the Field of Management." *Academy of Management Perspectives* 26 no. 3, pp.12–21.

Mas, I., D. Radcliffe. 2010. *Mobile Payments Go Viral: M-PESA in Kenya.* http://siteresources.worldbank.org/AFRICAEXT/Resources/258643-1271798012256/M-PESA_Kenya.pdf (accessed November 4, 2017).

Mercy Corps Nepal. 2008. *Mercy Corps Nepal Microfinance Assessment: Scope of Meso-level Technical Service Provision to MFIs in Nepal.* http://nepal .mercycorps.org/pdf/Mercy Corps Nepal Micro Finance Assessment Scope of Meso Level Technical Service Provisionto MFIs in Nepal.pdf (accessed November 4, 2017).

Mohammad, G., and R.D. Yunaningsih. 2014. "Lessons from Informal Financial Systems: Indonesian Perspective." http://blog.microsave.net/lessons-from -informal-financial-systems-indonesian-perspective/ (accessed November 4, 2017).

Porter, M.E., and M.R. Kramer. 2011. "Creating Shared Value." *Harvard Business Review* 89, no. 1, pp. 62–77.

Rippey, P., and B. Fowler. 2011. *Beyond Financial Services: A Synthesis of Studies on the Integration of Savings Groups and Other Developmental Activities.* Geneva: Aga Khan Foundation.

Rutherford, S., and S.S. Arora. 2009. *The Poor and Their Money: Microfinance from a Twenty-first Century Consumer's Perspective.* Warwickshire: Practical Action Publishing.

Singh, S. 2013. *Globalization and Money: A Global South Perspective.* Lanham: Rowman & Littlefield Publishers.

Srinivas, H. n.d. *A Typology of Informal Credit Suppliers: Moneylenders.* http:// www.gdrc.org/icm/suppliers/typ-ml.html (accessed November 4, 2017).

Thompson, N.A. 2014. "Short-term Loans and Long-term Benefits: Tandas are" No-interest, Short-term Loans that Can Help Latina Entrepreneurs and Job-creators. *Latin Post.* http://www.latinpost.com/articles/10321/20140410/ short-term-loans-benefits-latinas-tandas-no-interest-loans-latina-entrepreneurs-job-creators.htm (accessed November 4, 2017).

Tsai, K.S. 2004. *Back-alley Banking: Private Entrepreneurs in China.* Ithaca: Cornell University Press.

US AID. 2008. *Nepal Inclusive Economic Growth Assessment: Microenterprise Development.* http://pdf.usaid.gov/pdf_docs/PNADN015.pdf (accessed November 4, 2017).

CHAPTER 9

Birth and Growth in Isolation

Development of the Generic Pharmaceutical Industry in Bangladesh

Md. Noor Un Nabi and Utz Dornberger

Introduction

The pharmaceutical industry in developed countries has been occupying a complex and critical role in the public healthcare system since the era of colonization until globalization. Poor countries welcomed the arrival of drug preparation from pharmaceutical industries in developed countries as a fundamental resource to promote basic healthcare, prevent diseases, and manage public health emergencies. State-of-the-art knowledge and technology and high cost of entry in the modern pharmaceutical industry promise (near) monopoly for leading companies in their markets (Gabriel 2014). This is an industry with a global span of economic power (Williams et al. 2008) where nation states, irrespective of the status of development, have been seen to struggle with. With the renewed momentum of globalization under World Trade Organization (WTO), the position of the pharmaceutical industry in the globalization discussion has been related to right to healthcare at the global level, qualitative and continuous advancement in healthcare through innovation, and an incentive system development for innovation and advancement in the pharmaceutical industry (Cullet 2003).

With the implementation of WTO charter in 2000, member countries agreed on Trade-Related Aspects of Intellectual Property Rights (TRIPS) for protecting the rights of the inventor and originators of intellectual contents in global trade. The pharmaceutical industry is the most featured industry in the discussion of the impacts of TRIPS. Here, member states generally agreed that pharmaceutical product and process patents should be granted and enforced by trade among member states. TRIPS has been received with welcome from the pharmaceutical transnational corporations (TNCs) and countries concerned, as according to their views, developing countries and global public health stand to benefit (Hoen 2002). Nevertheless, suspicion and concerns relating to the promised benefits of TRIPS have been voiced out. On the one hand, they relate to the deepening of health woes of already beleaguered developing countries. On the other hand, they relate to further increase in power of TNCs, which may induce more inequality at the global level (Kerry and Lee 2007).

Against this backdrop, this chapter presents the development of a modern pharmaceutical industry in Bangladesh since 1982 when the government promulgated Drug Ordinance 1982 in order to hold back pharmaceutical TNCs in Bangladesh.

Emergence of the Generic Pharmaceutical Industry in Bangladesh

Highly import-based healthcare system is always a complex and costly venture for poor countries. Pharmaceutical TNCs are accused of unfair and sometimes unethical practices, for example, marketing drugs with misrepresented therapeutic value (Kessler et al. 1994), dumping (Breckenridge 1986), marketing drug of little therapeutic value (Jayasuriya 1981), and unethical profit targeting, drug promotion, and marketing (Jayasuriya 1981; Kessel 2014) in developing countries. Being pushed in the 1970s by the ever-rising cost of healthcare amid oil- and war-induced shocks in global economy, coupled with the increasing concerns of activists and leaders about questionable business practices of the TNCs in the developing countries, some countries, for example, India, Pakistan, Sri Lanka, Chile, and Afghanistan, initiated reforms in their pharmaceutical sectors by installing regulatory instruments in order to secure more public health benefit with less cost burden (Chowdhury 2006). Responding to repeated calls WHO published and urged greater and affordable access to the list of essential drugs for developing countries in 1977. Being compelled by the socioeconomic context and demand from the activists, the Bangladesh government took initiatives to draw a full-fledged drug policy suitable to support the affordable and improved quality of healthcare. The Bangladesh government in accordance with the recommendations of an expert committee promulgated the "Drug Ordinance and Control (DOC) 1982." The key features of this ordinance (Chowdhury 1995; Ahmed 2002) include:

1. 1,742 drugs prevalent in the market, majority of which were either produced or imported in Bangladesh by TNCs, were identified as nonessential or therapeutically nonsignificant and their production and distribution were banned.

2. 150 drugs were listed as essential and lifesaving and 100 drugs as specialized drugs. Their price was to be set and controlled by the government.

3. Production and distribution of combination drugs were banned generally.

4. Production and distribution of products of doubtful, little, or no therapeutic value, and rather sometimes harmful and subject to misuse were banned.

5. Drugs manufactured with only a slight difference in composition from another product but having similar action were disallowed.

6. The importation of a finished drug, raw material or its close substitute that was produced in the country with the exact composition, or a close substitute was disallowed if the drugs are produced by the local manufacturers and supply was sufficient in the local market.

7. Multinational companies were encouraged to concentrate only on producing innovative and high therapeutic value drugs in Bangladesh.

8. No foreign brands were to be manufactured under license in any factory in Bangladesh if the same or similar products were available /manufactured in Bangladesh.

9. No multinational company without their own factory in Bangladesh would be allowed to market their products after manufacturing them in another factory in Bangladesh on a toll basis.

DOC 1982 was resisted by medical practitioners in Bangladesh and by the pharmaceutical TNCs worldwide. Foreign governments and the legislative bodies including the US Congress and the German Bundestag asked the Bangladesh government not to enforce it considering the freedom of choice of the medical practitioners, consumers' right, and business freedom (Chowdhury 1995). At the same time, DOC 1982 was hailed by the different rights groups, philanthropic bodies, and the professional organizations in Bangladesh and abroad. The Bangladesh government did not rescind the DOC 1982 and this legislation became the critical turning point of the local pharmaceutical industry development in Bangladesh (Reich, 1994).

Growth under the Protective Regime of the DOC 1982

Before 1982, the local pharmaceutical market was dominated by the TNCs largely by their imports and few production by local subsidiaries, while the role of local companies was truly insignificant (Begum 2007; Chowdhury 1995). The DOC 1982 reduced the operational scope and profit possibility of TNCs, forcing them to withdraw from Bangladesh. In many cases of withdrawal TNCs sold their business to their local management. Local entrepreneurs started investing in this sector sensing the availability of skilled human resources raised by the TNCs, a protected domestic market with huge population, and a high prevalence rate of disease and government incentives (Nabi 2010).

Currently, the local industry produces 95 percent of its annual need of generic human medicine for its 160 million people and the 5 percent import constitutes only state-of-the art medicines. The industry consists of 258 registered allopathic pharmaceutical manufacturers producing 1,268 generic preparations under 23,568 brand names (Directorate General of Drug Administration Bangladesh 2016). Domestic market has grown from a mere US $222 million in 1982 to US $1,353 million in 2014, and it is expected to grow to US $4,059 million by 2024 (Begum 2007; Rahman 2015b; Nabi and Dornberger 2013). The expected average yearly growth in the next 5 years is 15 percent per year (Rahman 2017). Ninety percent of market share is controlled by the local manufacturers, while TNCs have 10 percent market share (www.export.gov 2016). In 1981, seven out of the top 10 companies in the domestic market were TNCs.

In 2016, all the top 10 companies are locally owned and managed companies (Lincoln and Bhattacharjee 2007; Bhadra 2017). The Bangladeshi pharmaceutical industry started indirectly exporting their products to neighboring countries including Myanmar, Nepal, and Sri Lanka. The industry started direct export in 1992 when BEXIMCO, a leading company, exported Active Pharmaceutical Ingredient (API) to Hong Kong (Lincoln and Bhattacharjee 2007). The collapse of Soviet Union in 1991 encouraged Bangladeshi pharmaceutical manufacturers to penetrate European markets by accessing Eastern Europe with some initial successes (Begum 2007; Nabi 2010). In 2017, the Bangladeshi industry exported finished generics of different preparations and delivery forms, antiretroviral (HIV) drugs, inhalers, and vaccines to 127 countries (The Daily Star 2017). Its export market mainly constitutes countries where regulations are minimum to moderate, while few exports enter into highly and strictly regulated markets (Kathuria and Malouche 2016). The export figure is yet to reach US $100 million against the increasing number of markets. In the last 7 years, export grew at a rate of 25 percent and the industry projects that in the next 5 years export may reach US $1 billion (The Daily Star 2017). If the industry wants to achieve this ambitious target, it has to focus on making significant progress in the highly regulated markets. It is imperative for the industry to upgrade technological and management capabilities. The country's institutions must improve their capability and efficiency in addressing the industry's policy, infrastructure, and service needs. Besides direct export, leading Bangladeshi pharmaceutical companies are engaged in "contract manufacturing" for the foreign firms in international markets (Nabi 2010).

TRIPS, Global Healthcare, and Pharmaceutical Industry of Bangladesh

Among other outcomes of the Doha round of negotiation, WTO members agreed to formulate or reform their national laws relating to Intellectual Property Rights (IPR) protection and appropriate enforcement system. These are to avoid trade discrimination in the domestic industry and to boost international trade among member states. This agreement is generally known as TRIPS. WTO members also agreed to ratify and incorporate other existing treaties relating to the protection of IPR in their respective national laws. Article 27.1 of TRIPS states that patent shall be available for any invention, inventive step, and industrial application of intellectual exertions. Article 33 suggests that the term of patent protection should not be less than 20 years from the date of filing the patent application. Article 41 states that enforcement mechanisms must be capable of discharging effective action against current and future acts of patent infringement (Azam 2017). TRIPS in developing countries context spurred discussions due to a number of concerns:

1. Patent protection may increase the cost of production of the medicines and put constraints on availability and affordability in poor countries (Lanjouw 2005).
2. Obligatory product patent protection may open the floodgate of emergence of low counterfeit and quality drugs (Pécoul et al. 1999).
3. Universal patent protection may discourage TNCs in Research and Development (R&D) and investment in improving existing drugs for common diseases like malaria, etc. (Pogge 2014).

Article 31 of TRIPS addresses the case of public health emergency concern of poor countries by authorizing national agencies to revoke the right of the patent holder unilaterally for handling the condition. Nevertheless, authorities may be constrained to implement it (Agovino 2001). Some optimism relating to TRIPS has been voiced out since it impacts price and drug accessibility in poor countries. TRIPS may facilitate increased availability of substitutes to poor countries and encourage extensive technology transfer from developed to developing countries (Chaudhuri et al. 2003; Greer et al. 2006).

The Bangladeshi pharmaceutical industry is enjoying the second phase of the patent compliance waiver until 2033 as a member of Least Developed Countries group in pursuance with Article 65 and 66 of the TRIPS. During this period Bangladesh has to amend and reformulate its patent law (The Design and Patent Act 1911) in harmonization with TRIPS as well as to develop an effective enforcement system. Currently, Patent Act 1911 does not consider any patent provision for pharmaceutical products. In a TRIPS-compliant regime, it will be required to allow a

20 years' patent for the pharmaceutical product. The provisions for compulsory licensing, parallel import, strict patentability criteria, and R&D should be the other major integration in the TRIPS-compliant patent regime (Azam 2017). The following trade- and production-related provisions of DOC 1982 have to be streamlined by Bangladesh in order to enter into TRIPS-compliant regime in 2034:

1. All types of import restriction from pharmaceutical finished products and raw materials should be lifted.
2. All types of production opportunities should be allowed to foreign companies in all the branches of the industry.
3. Combined ingredient drugs should be allowed.
4. Price control should be lifted.
5. Restriction on advertising the pharmaceutical products should be lifted.

Such amendments will change the functional dynamics of the industry by removing the protection for local companies. Amid the discontent of industry and the activists, the National Drug Policy 2016 has approved FDI, contract manufacturing and licensing opportunities for the foreign companies in Bangladesh, and joint venture with foreign companies for producing finished drugs and API (National Drug Policy 2016).

The Bangladesh pharmaceutical industry and healthcare sector is yet to face any adverse effects of patents due to two primary reasons. Firstly, the industry has been continuously increasing its manufacturing capabilities in diversified classes of drugs for retaining their competitiveness in the domestic market. Secondly, the dominant part of the local market demand is constituted by the need for off-patented generic drug (Azam 2017).

Taking Bangladeshi Pharmaceutical Industry in the TRIPS-Compliant Regime

One of the key issues for the Bangladeshi Pharmaceutical industry in the TRIPS-compliant regime is to decrease its excessive dependency on imported API. The biggest benefit the Bangladeshi pharmaceutical industry can add to the development of its long-term competitiveness during the TRIPS waiver period is to enhance its capability of API production (Van Duzer 2003). Since 2008, the Bangladesh government and the industry's efforts in this regard are yet to be functional. In a TRIPS-compliant regime, it is imperative for the Bangladeshi industry to enhance its R&D capacity, at least to the level of enhancing drug reverse engineering capability than only focusing on generic formulations manufacturing. Reverse engineering may allow Bangladeshi manufacturers to get domestic "process patent," which may help them to secure their domestic market. Lack of government innovation incentives, arrangements, and frameworks for integrating university, research institutions, and firms for R&D purposes, and weaker government–firm technology transfer framework are bottlenecks impeding R&D capacity building in this industry (Sampath 2007). Recently Bangladeshi pharmaceutical manufacturers started heavily investing in process improvement for securing international certifications to break into the international markets in a significant manner. The biggest requirement consists of making the national watchdog and enforcement agency, Directorate General of Drug Administration (DGDA), capable of effective monitoring and enforcement. In terms of quantity and quality of knowledge and technological resources and facilities, DGDA does not meet the current needs of the booming domestic pharmaceutical industry (Azam 2017). Only one of the two drug testing and certification laboratories functions effectively, but this is too little to meet the needs of the domestic industry. Modern testing facilities including the bioequivalence testing and clinical trial facilities are yet to be developed in the country. DGDA is expected to play a strong monitoring and enforcing role which was not significantly visible during the first phase of TRIPS waiver 2006–2016 (Rahman 2015a). Fake and low-quality drugs have a dominant presence in rural parts of the domestic market, since producers avoid following Good Manufacturing Practice and sometimes operate without manufacturing license (The News Today 2016). In a TRIPS-compliant regime, this problem can be even more complex as importation of drugs cannot be restricted.

Conclusion

Bangladesh has set an extraordinary example of gaining good health at a very low cost and has been proposed as a role model for other developing countries in the region (Ahmed and Naheed 2015). Life expectancy at birth increased to 72 years in 2016 from 58.4 years in 1990, infant mortality per 1,000 live birth has dropped to 30.7 from 99.7 in 1990 (Human Development Report 2016). Among six countries including Bangladesh, Brazil, Malawi, Nepal, Sri Lanka, and Pakistan, for 32 selected essential medicines (both generic and innovator) in the private sector, affordability is highest on average in Bangladesh as well as in the private sector; the cost of treatment of selected noncommunicable diseases is the lowest in Bangladesh (Mendis et al. 2007). The epidemiological profile of Bangladesh has experienced significant shift during the 2005–2015 period, all age mortality per 100,000 people from communicable diseases, neonatal, maternal, and nutritional disorders has reduced significantly, whereas increase in death rate from noncommunicable diseases and injuries is on the rise (Wang et al. 2016). Health Assurance Quality Index of Bangladesh healthcare has improved to 51.7 in 2015 from 31.7 in 1990 (Institute of Health Metric and Evaluation 2015). A modern pharmaceutical industry in Bangladesh based on DOC 1982 has significantly contributed to such achievement. How the industry will function and contribute to the public health interest of Bangladesh in a post-2034 TRIPS-compliant regime depends on how far the industry and the local institutions can adjust according to the opportunities and challenges brought by TRIPS. Emergence and growth of the Bangladeshi pharmaceutical industry may not be replicable for the other developing countries due to WTO regulations. Yet the case of the Bangladeshi pharmaceutical industry adds to the evidence that competent protection measures help develop the base for industrial development. In addition, phased and strategic liberalization leads to benefits of such protections and follows the growth path of many developed nations (Chang 2003).

References

Agovino, T. 2001. "Companies Fear Precedent as They Cut AIDS Drug Prices for Africa." April 20. https://www.hks.harvard.edu/cidinthenews/article/ap_042001.html.

Ahmed, M. 2002. *Effects of Regulation in Pharma Market in Bangladesh*. Bangladesh Health Economics Conference at Hotel Sheraton, Dhaka.

Ahmed, S.M., and A. Naheed. 2015. "Bangladesh Health System Review." *Health Systems in Transition* 5, no. 3. Geneva: World Health Organization.

Azam, M. Monirul. 2017. "The impacts of TRIPS on the Pharmaceutical Regulation and Pricing of Drugs in Bangladesh." *International Journal of Law and Management* 59, no. 3, pp. 376–393. doi:10.1108/IJLMA-01-2016-0002.

Breckenridge, A.M.. 1986. "The Pharmaceutical Industry and Developing Countries." *British Journal of Clinical Pharmacology* 22 (S1).

Begum, R. 2007. "Pharmaceutical Industry: Potentials and Possibilities." *NDC (National Defense College Bangladesh) Journal* 6, no. 1, pp. 73–79.

Bhadra, C. 2017. "Pharmaceutical Industry - a Promising Sector." *The Financial Express*.http://www.thefinancialexpress-bd.com/2017/01/09/58657/Pharmaceutical-industry---a-promising-sector (accessed July 13, 2017).

Chang, H.-J. 2003. *Kicking Away the Ladder: Development Strategy in Historical Perspective*. Anthem studies in development and globalization. London: Anthem Press.

Chaudhuri, S., P. Goldberg, and P. Jia. 2003. *Estimating the Effects of Global Patent Protection in Pharmaceuticals: A Case Study of Quinolones in India*. Cambridge: National Bureau of Economic Research.

Chowdhury, F. 2006. "A Strategy for Establishing the API Park." Consultant Report.

Chowdhury, Z. 1995. *The Politics of Essential Drugs: The Makings of a Successful Health Strategy: Lessons from Bangladesh*. London: Atlantic Highlands, N.J. Zed Books.

Cullet, P. 2003. "Patents and Medicines: The Relationship between TRIPS and the Human Right to Health." *International Affairs* 79, no. 1, pp. 139–160. doi:10.1111/1468-2346.00299.

Directorate General of Drug Administration Bangladesh. 2016. Accessed August 01, 2017. http://www.dgda.gov.bd/index.php/faqs.

Gabriel, J.M. 2014. *Medical Monopoly: Intellectual Property Rights and the Origins of the Modern Pharmaceutical Industry*. Chicago: The University of Chicago Press.

Greer, J.M., P.K. Goldberg, and P. Jia. 2006. "Estimating the effects of global patent protection in pharmaceuticals: a case study of quinolones in India." *The American Economic Review* 96, no. 5, pp. 1477–1514.

Hoen, E. 2002. "TRIPS, Pharmaceutical Patents, and Access to Essential Medicines: a Long Way from Seattle to Doha." *Chicago Journal of International Law* 3, no. 1, pp. 27–46.

Human Development Report. 2016. *Human Development for Everyone 2016*. New York: United Nations Development Programme.

Institute of Health Metric and Evaluation. 2015. "How Does Personal Healthcare Access and Quality Measure up Against What Is Considered "Best Possible"? http://www.healthdata.org/bangladesh.

Jayasuriya, D.C. 1981. "Third World Strategies for Regulating Drug Advertising and Marketing." *Journal of Consumer Policy* 5, no. 3, pp. 287–262.

Kathuria, S., and M. Malouche. 2016. *Attracting Investment in Bangladesh—Sectoral Analyses: A Diagnostic Trade Integration Study.* Directions in development. Trade. Washington, D.C.: World Bank Group.

Kerry, V.B., and K. Lee. 2007. "TRIPS, the Doha Declaration and Paragraph 6 Decision: What Are the Remaining Steps for Protecting Access to Medicines?" *Globalization and Health* 3, p. 3.doi:10.1186/1744-8603-3-3.

Kessel, M. 2014. "Restoring the Pharmaceutical Industry's Reputation." *Nature Biotechnology* 32, no. 10, pp. 983–90. doi:10.1038/nbt.3036.

Kessler, D.A., J.L. Rose, R.J. Temple, R. Schapiro, and J.P. Griffin. 1994. "Therapeutic-Class Wars--Drug Promotion in a Competitive Marketplace." *New England Journal of Medicine* 331, no. 20: pp. 1350–1353.

Lanjouw, J. 2005. *Patents, Price Controls, and Access to New Drugs: How Policy Affects Global Market Entry.* Cambridge, MA: National Bureau of Economic Research.

Lincoln, Z., and H. Bhattacharjee. 2007. "Pharmaceutical Industry in Bangladesh: Structure, Performance and Future Strategies." *The Business and Economic Review* 11, no. 1, pp. 2–13.

Mendis, S., K. Fukino, R. Liang, A. Filipe Jr, O. Khatib, J. Lewoski, and M. Ewen. 2007. "The Availability and Affordability of Selected Essential Medicines for Chronic Diseases in Six Low- and Middle-Income Countries." *Bulletin of the World Health Organization* 85, no. 4: 279–288. doi:10.2471/BLT.06.033647.

Nabi, Md. N.U. 2010. "Dynamics of Internationalization of Firms: A Study of Pharmaceutical Exporters from Bangladesh." Doctoral Dissertation, Leipzig University. http://www.gko.uni-leipzig.de/forschung/promotionen/abgeschlossene-promotionen/2001-2010.html.

Nabi, Md. N.U., and U. Dornberger. 2013. "Entrepreneurship and the Institutional Context: Dynamics of Development of the Locally Owned Generic Pharmaceutical Industry in Bangladesh." In H. Etemad, T.K. Madsen, E.S. Rasmussen, and P. Servais (eds.) *Current Issues in International Entrepreneurship.* Cheltenham: Edward Elgar, pp. 199–240.

"National Drug Policy 2016." In *Bangladesh Gazette.* https://www.dgda.gov.bd/index.php/2013-03-31-05-16-29/guidance-documents/205-national-drug-policy-2017-with-essential-drug-list-and-otc-list.

Pécoul, B., P. Chirac, P. Trouiller, and J. Pinel. 1999. "Access to Essential Drugs in Poor Countries: a Lost Battle?" *JAMA* 281, no. 4, pp. 361–367.

Pogge, T. 2014. "Could Globalisation Be Good for World Health?" Global Justice: Theory Practice Rhetoric, Volume 1. Global Justice: Theory Practice Rhetoric, Volume 1. doi:10.21248/gjn.1.0.5.

Rahman, A.H.M.M. 2015a. "WTO Decision on Pharma: an Opportunity." *The Daily Star.* http://www.thedailystar.net/business/global-business/wto-decision-pharma-opportunity-174415 (accessed July 12, 2017).

Rahman, Md F. 2015b. "Pharma Sales to Treble by 2024: London-based BMI Research Forecasts." http://www.thedailystar.net/business/pharma-sales-treble-2024-183103 (accessed July 12, 2017).

Rahman, Md F. 2017. "Pharma Sector to Grow at 15pc a Year: Study." *The Daily Star.* http://www.thedailystar.net/business/pharma-sector-grow-15pc-year-study-1429024 (accessed July 12, 2017).

Reich, M.R. 1994. "Bangladesh Pharmaceutical Policy and Politics." *Health policy and planning* 9, no. 2, pp. 130-143.

Sampath, P.G. 2007. *Innovation and Competitive Capacity in Bangladesh's.* ISSN 1871-9872: United Nations University. http://www.merit.unu.edu/publications/working-papers/abstract/?id=3005 (accessed August 01, 2017).

The Daily Star. 2017. "Pharma sector can earn $1b in exports within five years: Industry people reiterate, call for incentives." March 29. Star Business Report. http://www.thedailystar.net/business/pharma-sector-can-earn-1b-exports-within-five-years-1383007 (accessed July 12, 2017).

The News Today. 2016. "Fake drug business rampant." http://newstoday.com.bd/index.php?option=details&news_id=2434981&date=2016-02-10 (accessed August 01, 2017).

Van Duzer, T. 2003. "TRIPS and the Pharmaceutical Industry in Bangladesh: Towards a National Strategy." *Centre for Policy Dialogue (CPD), Occasional Papers.*

Wang, H., M. Naghavi, C. Allen, R.M. Barber, Z.A. Bhutta, A. Carter, D.C. Casey, et al. 2016. "Global, Regional, and National Life Expectancy, All-cause Mortality, and Cause-specific Mortality for 249 Causes of Death, 1980–2015: A Systematic Analysis for the Global Burden of Disease Study 2015." *The Lancet* 388, no. 10053, pp. 1459–1544. doi:10.1016/S0140-6736(16)31012-1.

Williams, S.J., J. Gabe, and P. Davis. 2008. "The Sociology of Pharmaceuticals: Progress and Prospects." *Sociology of Health & Illness* 30, no. 6, pp. 813–824. doi:10.1111/j.1467-9566.2008.01123.x.

www.export.gov. 2016. *Bangladesh Pharmaceuticals.* https://www.export.gov/apex/article2?id=Bangladesh-Pharmaceutical (accessed August 01, 2017).

CHAPTER 10

Buy Local

A Consumer's Alternative to the Global Market?

Shelly Daly

Introduction

By now, most people worldwide have become familiar with the heart-felt marketing campaigns that urge us to support neighborhood shops, producers, and service providers and the lure is to pull consumers back from the global market and into the smaller local realm. Politicians have won and lost office based on their ability to support and reinforce their local economy and business councils and entrepreneurship programs are thriving in universities and cities. However, consumers are finding large international brands of clothing in these neighborhood shops and exotic nonindigenous produce in markets and they are beginning to wonder what it means to buy "local" and whether being "unglobal" is just a myth or an achievable reality.

The "Buy Local" Campaign

Consumers have always had a varying array of buying choices and, in most markets, an abundance of information to help make that choice. Low cholesterol, fair trade, sustainable, low sodium, and organic are just a few of the well-known and universally used notations to lure customers into a purchase decision. Locally grown and buy-local are just the newest variations of information decision-making tools available to consumers of food and nonfood items. There does not seem to be a universal or legal definition of what these terms mean and news reports, grocers, and retail shops can basically interpret and use these terms in a variety of ways known to and defined independently by them on any given day. A 2007 study (Turner 2007) found that 30 percent of consumers were not even sure what the terms meant and whether they should be buying organic fare or locally grown fare. The last decade has not brought much clarification at any level of the supply chain or purchase point. The assertion to buy local may in itself be misleading and an *Alice In Wonderland*-like rabbit hole. If you live in Indiana, does "buy local" mean you get avocadoes from California instead of Mexico? Or does it mean that the avocadoes are from within a 5-mile range? Is local the same as organic? Consumers are free to interpret and question but do those end retailers always know the answer? If the avocadoes are grown organically, does that mean they are also shipped organically from California or Mexico all the way to Indiana or did the shipper add pesticide in order to preserve them once harvested and packed to move across a continent?

Politicians and Governments

New York councilman Rafael Slamanca Jr. in an article by Hu (2016) made a public proclamation of his goal to buy local products connected to the South Bronx neighborhood he represented. It made news in one of the most reputable papers in the United States, the *New York Times*. Such efforts are not isolated events and most consumers can recall a time when they heard, read, or saw an endorsement or similar proclamation.

Similarly, the national government of the United Kingdom has spent more than a decade encouraging consumers to buy locally produced food (Chambers et al. 2007). The encouragement was rooted in the government goals of sustainability and the hope and motivation in the efforts extended as far as providing an impetus for economic, environmental, and social benefits.

The European Union (EU) has a "Protected Food Name Scheme" and member states are encouraged to use this fact in stimulating consumers to buy local and traditional foods in their regions. Any producer of food which is based on specific regional or traditional recipes can apply to protect the name of that food based on the EU's wording in the protocol.

The idea was to communicate to consumers a level of trust and quality in the origin of the food and to take advantage of consumers' desire to support local industry and business. George Streatfield (Stock 2006) states that this has created an ability for charging premium prices and that "Locally sourced and traditionally made products could be perceived as a new kind of designer label." He goes on to state, "There's a really strong story to tell . . . and this will ultimately draw sales and be a catalyst for supermarkets to stock more" of the locally grown products protected by the EU wording.

Tony Blair's election to lead Great Britain came with a first speech replete with pride and an emphasis on being the "best" country for living in, raising children in, and growing old in (Freedman 1998). It was a rally cry to focus on the nation at a time when the rest of the world was in discourse over globalization. Hall (1992) stated that culture was and would continue to regulate globalization and this seems to be the case despite the mass media and internet influence on homogenizing tastes.

Jersey City Small Business Services in the state of New Jersey, with the support and endorsement of the city's mayor, launched a yearlong campaign in December of 2016 encouraging residents to "Shop Jersey City, Buy Local." "Small businesses reflect who we are as a city and our unique diversity" stated the mayor (Barker 2016). Barker stated that 6,000 new jobs and 450 new small businesses opened in Jersey City between July 2013 and December 2016. The mayor's efforts are seen as a direct and vital link to sustaining the local economy and continued growth in small and medium-sized enterprises.

Nongovernment Promoters of Buy Local

Bountiful Colorado is an example of a nongovernment agency promoting consumers to buy local foods. They have developed educational material, ads, and displays in order to tell consumers where and when to buy locally grown products and were assisted in their efforts by nutritionists and farmers. When surveyed, 86 percent of consumers agreed with the stated reasons for purchasing local products as included in the Bountiful Colorado materials (Savage and Auld 2006). Many states across the United States and many rural communities, subdivisions, and neighborhoods across the vast expanse of the country have implemented and used similar appeals and programs to assist consumers in sourcing local foods. In Kansas City, Missouri, news channels regularly identified and shared such information such as the independently produced blog created by Mike and Laurie Snell, "KC Raised" (www.kcraised.com).

The trend for appealing to consumers based on local appeal goes as far back as 1996 even in post-Soviet Russia (McKay 1996) where businesses attempted to change their image to appeal to consumer enthusiasm and ongoing patriotism. The USSR and post-Soviet states of the former USSR were universally engaged in a pursuit of all things foreign and especially the heavily banned American made products. After the disintegration of the USSR into many independent areas and countries, the door seemed to be open to nationalistic pride in not just the largest of the new states, but also in those newly independent countries whose personal story and cultural identity had long been suppressed under the umbrella of the USSR. Nationalistic pride was most easily attained and touted through the promotion and promulgation of local foods, products, and sourcing.

The Assumptions Behind Buying Local

Shorter Supply Chain, Lower Costs

Sullivan et al. (2013) examined consumers' use of agricultural product information sources and their shopping outlet patronage preferences for one type of locally grown produce: avocados. These researchers identified two farmers' market segments as people who shop only at farmers' markets and those who cross-shops at farmer's markets and grocery stores. In their study, product information came from a variety of sources including media, retailers, and organizations. They then evaluated produce shopping decisions through the use of "buy local" and "product origin." The "buy local" information was found to be a significant source of information for the segment of consumers who shopped at farmer's markets.

When politicians promote the idea of locally based purchases, there is often the touted advantage of lower costs due to a shorter distance between producer and consumer. However, quite often, the limited supply and labor-intensive practice of growing, harvesting, and selling their own products actually translate to higher costs at farmers' markets throughout the country. So it seems that although "buy local" may mean a shorter supply chain or a system where one person or one business assumes multiple roles in that chain, consumers are willing to pay a premium for the inherent appeal behind buying local. This appeal may be the ability to support their community, fresher products, or higher degree of knowledge about the food's source and growing conditions. Research has not yet fully identified why consumers are willing to pay more, but the reasons are undoubtedly many and varied.

Camaraderie

The idea of shopping local in order to increase cohesion of a community or ethnic identity is also prevalent in the impetus to buy local. The phenomenon is seen from the weekend markets in Los Angeles, California, and New York City, to Eau Claire, Wisconsin, and its Hong Chinese ethnic market, to rural Chinese markets (Roussillat 2014) in mainland China and as far as the twenty districts of the remote regions of Bhutan.

The Central Coast Grown association began in 2011 developing and distributing farmer trading cards in an effort to encourage consumers to connect with, get to know, and support local farmers (Eddy 2013). The New England states launched a campaign "Be a Local Hero, Buy Locally Grown" campaign to encourage a social response and to economically boost the region.

In Israel, the idea of "buy local" was not directed against imports but rather was a movement to "Buy Jewish" by attributing ethnic qualities to objects in order to define them as Jewish or, alternatively, foreign, which reflected economic conflict and political conceptions of Jewish identity (Shoham 2013).

Overcoming Obstacles in Buying Local

The obstacles and deterrents to buy local are numerous. For example, a study by Chambers et al. (2007) found that buying local was perceived as less convenient and costlier in terms of price. Despite this, respondents throughout a UK -based study were enthusiastic to buy greater degrees and quantities of local products and foods. In looking at the government campaign, Certified South Carolina Grown, used to encourage local consumption, Hughes and Isengildina-Massa (2015) found there was no contribution to the state's economy. Alternatively, Prall (2013) reported that local economies were bolstered during major holiday seasons when governments supported and pushed "buy local" campaigns. Prall's report stated a positive response from business owners and bolstered sales revenues.

Parts and Vida (2008) found that more cosmopolitan consumers tended to purchase foreign-made products. Their work stemmed from five decades of country-of-origin studies and factors influencing consumer choice. However, Blake et al. (2010) found that buying local involved an understanding of convenience, health, and status for respondents in their research. These consumers found that the number of miles their food traveled was just one more aspect of an element to consider alongside cost, quality, and availability.

Convenience foods could be argued as the antithesis of buying local. Gilliland et al. (2015) researched the use of a phone app to encourage improved dietary behavior and its ability to draw people to local food vendors at a greater frequency. Their study is intriguing in consideration of health benefits associated with the "buy local" ideology but also in considering the plague of packaged and processed foods as the ultimate enemy to build local consumption.

Is Buying Local the Opposite of Globalization?

Climate change concerns have focused on the push to reduce the distance food travels as part of the effort to sustain and nurture environment. Buying local not only decreased the lengthy distribution path that often involves copious amounts of fuel consumption and pollution, but it also inherently builds on the belief in most consumer's minds that products are grown with more sustainable methods and fewer environment-damaging chemicals.

Pack (2011) found that consumption of global media actually heightened group identity and decreased homogenization of Navaho culture. Pack went on to comment that cultural transfer is never met with total or indiscriminate acceptance and that despite attempts within various forms of media to influence and lure consumers to a product or lifestyle choice, it can cause the opposite effect. When the media lure inundates a cultural ideology, such as that of the Navaho nation in Pack's study, the viewers actually had an opposite of expected response by finding higher value and greater effort into preserving what was unique, and not represented in media, as their own idea of culture.

While it is hard to define and agree on exactly what buying local means, it can safely be argued at this point that there is a need for viewing the "buy local" movement as something very different and unique from the lure of globalization. Research needs to ask, wonder, and eventually study whether part of the allure of "buy local" is the desire to preserve a community, culture, or way of life that has been systematically threatened over eight decades of increasing levels of big-box stores, internet shopping, and the overall trend of internationalization of product choices and purchase decisions.

"Buy local" may be the consumer's ultimate choice of something other than globalization. Whether most consumers would recognize this, or even voice such a position, is open for debate, but the argument and growing presence of the movement should cause us to consider the alternative presented through such efforts. Further study is needed to understand the strategic implications for large and multinational companies. The "buy local" ideology seems here to stay; it will not be the first challenge to increasing levels of globalization and it will not be immune to the inherent pressures of our global marketplace.

Buying local comes with its benefits and detractions. Buying local may mean higher prices or limited supply. The benefits of buying local as an alternative to globalization are evident and multilateral. The point at which this alternative and its benefits fail to satisfy a community, group, or culture will only be known in the future. For now, this option for globalization is growing and secure and appears to be here to stay.

References

Barker, C.J. 2016. *Campaign Launched in Jersey City Promotes Small Businesses during Holiday Season.* The New York Amsterdam News, 4 December.

Blake, M.K., J. Mellor, and L. Crane. 2010. "Buying Local Food: Shopping Practices, Place and Consumption Networks in Defining Food as "Local"." *Annals of the Association of American Geographers* 100, no. 2, pp. 409–426.

Chambers, S., A. Lobb, L. Butler, K. Harvey, B. Trail. 2007. "Local National and Imported Foods: A qualitative Study." *Appetite* 49, no. 1, pp. 208–213.

Eddy, D. 2013. "Farmer Trading Card." *American Fruit Grower* 133, no. 10, pp. 46–47.

Freedman, D. 1998. "Globalization and Local Consumption: the Labour Party's Attempts to Sell British Media." *Contemporary Politics* 4, no. 4, pp. 413–428.

Gilliland, J., R. Sadler, A. Clark, C. O'Connor, M. Milczarek and S. Doherty. 2015. "Using a Smartphone Application to Promote Healthy Dietary Behaviours and Local Food consumption." *BioMed Research International.* Hindawi Publishing Corporation, Volume 15.

Hall, S. 1992. "Cultural Studies and Its Theoretical Legacies." In L. Grossberg, C. Nelson, and P. Treichler (eds.) *Cultural Studies.* New York: Routledge, pp. 277–294.

Hu, W. 2016. "Buy Local? Newest Councilman Makes It His Mission." *New York Times* 165, no. 57155, pA19.

Hughes, D.W. and O. Isengildina-Massa. 2015. "The Economic Impact of Farmers' Markets and a State Level Locally Grown Campaign." *Food Policy* 54, pp. 78–84.

McKay, B. 1996. "In Russia, West No Longer Means Best." *Wall Street Journal – Eastern Edition,* Vol 228 Issue 113, p.A9.

Pack, S. 2011. "Global Transmission and Local Consumption: Navajo Resistance to Mainstream American Television'" *Journal of International & Global Studies,* Lindenwood University Press 2, no. 2, pp. 81–94.

Parts, O. and I. Vida. 2008. "The Effects of Consumer Cosmopolitanism on Purchase Behavior of Foreign vs. Domestic Products;" *Managing Global Transitions* 9, no. 4, pp. 355–370.

Prall, D. 2016. "Home for the Holidays" *American City and Country,* http://americancityandcounty.com/american-city-and-county?page=0%2C105

Roussillat, S. 2014. "Bazaar Day!" *China Today* 63, no. 2, p. 82.

Savage, A.L. and G.W. Auld. 2006. "Development and Evaluation of Educational Materials Promoting Local Colorado Foods." *Journal of Nutrition Education & Behavior* 38, no. 1, pp. 61–62.

Shoham, H. 2013. "Buy Local" or "Buy Jewish"? Separatist Consumption in Interwar Palestine." *International Journal of Middle East Studies* 45, no. 3, pp. 469–489.

Stocks, C. 2006. "EU 'name' Scheme Taps into Food Lifestyle Market." *Farmers Weekly* 145, no. 17.

Sullivan, P., C. Chan-Halbrendt, J. Krishnakumar. 2013. "Are Farmers' Market Shoppers Different From Cross-Shoppers? The Case of Hawaiian Avocado Purchasers." *Journal of Food Products Marketing* 19, no. 5, pp. 363–375.

Turner, L. 2007. "More Than Organic." *Vegetarian Times.*

Vanvranken, R. 2007. "Local" Is in the Eye of the Beholder." *American Vegetable Grower* 55, no. 3, p. 50.

SECTION 5

Conclusion

CHAPTER 11

Conclusion

J. Mark Munoz

Globalization has redefined traditional thinking about business, economics, and politics. It has forced organizations worldwide to reconfigure their organizations to adapt to a fast-changing and hypercompetitive environment. It has set the stage for a new economic order and in many ways flattened the world (Slaughter 2002; Friedman 2005).

Globalization contributed to trade expansion and growth in a number of multinational corporations and is widely believed to improve the movement of people, capital, goods, and information (Dicken 1998; PWC 2017). Some firms, however, have decided to evolve and reinvent themselves as they move along. Others decided to stay the course and maintain their old ways. Yet others decided to be "unglobal" and defined their own game.

The "unglobals" or individuals, companies, and countries who have decided to operate against the grain of traditional globalization have forged on a different path. They have decided to pursue an alternative pathway in a globalized world.

There are nations such as the United Kingdom that have voted to leave the European Union and voiced this viewpoint in a referendum known as Brexit (Britain Exit). In the United States, the citizens have opted to elect Donald Trump, a billionaire entrepreneur, who has embraced a populist and protectionist standpoint. Sweden has opted to implement protectionist measures, especially in the service sector (Krause 2009). Norway at one point imposed high import tariffs on cheese and meat (Bergland 2013). Many countries take on a similar approach using diverse means such as tariffs, subsidies, antidumping regulations, local content requirements, and "buy local" policies. A Nielsen (2009) report noted in a 52-country survey that almost half or 45 percent of consumers supported government efforts to put restraints on imports of foreign products.

Among companies, there are businesses that opt to stay away from international trade and channel all their efforts on the domestic market. For instance, in many developing nations one can see multitudes of microenterprises operating street stalls or farming and fishing communities selling products solely to local consumers. Global events and the notion of globalization are far detached from their minds and daily lives.

Among individuals, there are people who choose to live in complete isolation. A couple in Spain named Juan Martin Colomer and Sinforosa Sancho live off the grid in an abandoned mountain village in Aragon, Spain (Piegsa-Quischotte 2016). Pedro Luca has made a cave in northern Argentina his home for decades (Fox News 2016). While these are extreme cases of isolationism, it provides concrete evidence that not everyone desires to be globally linked. Some individuals choose to be excluded or have been excluded as a result of their geography, condition, or status in society.

There are mixed perceptions on the value of globalization. A PWC (2017) survey of CEOs noted that: (1) only 28 percent believed globalization averted climate change and resource scarcity, (2) only 35 percent believed it enhanced fairness in the integrity of the global tax system, and (3) only 44 percent believed it closed the gap between the rich and poor. In recent years, there has been a growing social movement comprised of individuals who support global cooperation and interaction, but do not favor the negative effects of economic globalization. This group action is called Alter-globalization (Pleyers 2010) and it aims to address negative global consequences relating to economic, political, cultural, social, and environmental issues.

This book featured cases and stories of alternative paths to globalization. There is evidence suggesting that unconventional approaches in dealing with globalization could be viable for some.

On the topic of countries and governance, it is noteworthy that a country like Bhutan has taken on an entirely different measure of development—happiness of its citizens rather than extensive globalization or rapid economic progress. This case suggests that countries need not follow parameters and benchmarks set by others, they have the right and privilege of living and governing in their own terms.

With regard to institutions and policies, the cases in this book suggest that in a large part international financial institutions yield much influence on countries and the world. Political and economic forces within and outside of a country shape the policies and direction pursued by a nation. Organizations need to carefully monitor these influencing forces and strategically navigate potential challenges. The case of the Karachaganak Petroleum Operating Consortium showed that doing business in Kazakhstan meant thinking global, but acting local. The formation of strong local partnerships and alliances can lead to success.

The featured cases illustrate that some businesses and industries may have found alternative pathways to globalization. Business entities in some emerging markets have thrived using informal and alternative banking initiatives. Other businesses directed their business development efforts to local consumers. These cases suggest that one does not always have to follow a global route in order to be successful.

The approaches mentioned in this book, however, are not "one size fits all" approaches. There are a multitude of factors that might make an approach work in one location, but fail in another. Political, social, economic and cultural factors among others will have an impact on the economic outcome.

Nevertheless, given the countless debates on the merits and demerits of globalization and the constant quest for answers on the challenges it brings, the cases and new ideas are worth exploring. These cases may indeed be the actual solution, or it may be a stepping stone toward the effective management of globalization.

The featured chapters suggest that it is worthwhile to be asking the right globalization questions. Table 11.1 showcases important questions that need to be asked.

Asking the right questions and creating a viable plan are important first steps in finding alternative pathways to globalization. Table 11.2 highlights important considerations for a Globalization Alternative Plan.

The creation of a Globalization Alternative Plan will help individuals and organizations, think through existing challenges and opportunities, and will improve the chances for a successful implementation.

Table 11.1 Key questions on globalization alternatives

Countries and Governance	What challenges and opportunities do countries face in a globalized environment? What are a country's strengths and weaknesses? How can these strengths be leveraged for success? What alternative globalization response options have not been considered? Why or why not? If these alternative options are pursued, what might the outcome be? What timelines and resources need to be considered? Who would execute the plan? What types of support would be essential? What are the best and worst case scenarios?
Institutions	What challenges and opportunities impact the institution in a globalized environment? What are the institution's strengths and weaknesses? How can these strengths be leveraged for success? What alternative globalization response options have not been considered? Why or why not? If these alternative options are pursued, what might the outcome be? What timelines and resources need to be considered? Who would execute the plan? What types of support would be essential? What are the best and worst case scenarios?
Policies	What challenges and opportunities impact current economic, business, and political policies in a globalized environment? What are the strengths and weaknesses of these policies? How can these be altered to achieve greater success? What alternative globalization response options have not been considered? Why or why not? If these alternative options are pursued, what might the outcome be? What timelines and resources need to be considered for policy changes? Who would execute the policy changes? What types of support would be essential? What are the best and worst case scenarios?
Businesses and Industries	What challenges and opportunities do organizations face in a globalized environment? What are the organization's strengths and weaknesses? How can these strengths be leveraged for success? What alternative globalization response options have not been considered? Why or why not? If these alternative options are pursued, what might the outcome be? What timelines and resources need to be considered? Who would execute the plan? What types of support would be essential? What are the best and worst case scenarios?
Individuals	What challenges and opportunities do I face in a globalized environment? What are my strengths and weaknesses? How can I leverage these strengths for success? What alternative globalization response options have I not considered? Why or why not? If these alternative options are pursued, what might the outcome be? What timelines and resources need to be considered? Who would execute the plan? What types of support would be essential? What are the best and worst case scenarios?

Table 11.2 Globalization alternative plan

Steps	Tasks	Action agenda
Step 1	Understand global and local environment	• Prepare a comprehensive research study on the global and local operational environment • In large organizations, a team brainstorming session or a steering committee might be helpful in getting the process started • Identify five global and five local issues that are critical for global success
Step 2	Assess strengths and weaknesses	• Assess personal or organizational strengths and weaknesses • Determine personal or organizational key competencies and competitive advantages
Step 3	Identify areas for strategic change	• Select three best options that best leverage personal or organizational strengths with the global environment
Step 4	Assess and analyze the viability of change	• Evaluate the three best options with considerations placed on its impact, ease of execution, resource needed, and timeline • Select the best option for globalization alternative
Step 5	Plan for the implementation of the change	• Create a comprehensive Globalization Alternative Plan with considerations placed on who will execute, resources needed, and timelines
Step 6	Determine standards and benchmarks	• Identify metrics for success as well as expected standards and benchmarks
Step 7	Implement the change	• Implement the Globalization Alternative Plan
Step 8	Review and update	• Review and update the plan based on global, local, operational, and competitive changes • Stay abreast with sociopolitical, economic, and business changes taking place locally and globally

Organizations need to stay in control of the internationalization process (Vermeulen 2001). Before deciding to go global companies need to understand what the benefits are, if necessary management skills are available, and if the costs will outweigh the benefits (Alexander and Korine 2008). Given the fast-changing nature of the global environment, periodic update and review of the Globalization Alternative Plan is essential.

Aside from having a Globalization Alternative Plan, the chapters in this book suggest that organizations would benefit from global receptiveness and a strong support structure. Ten key organizational attributes would enhance its effort in finding effective globalization alternative strategies.

1. **Global mindset** – high global interest and cross-cultural appreciation would lead to knowledge of international issues and would be helpful in organizational planning. In understanding globalization extent, organizations need to consider social, political, and economic implications (Dreher 2006). Management mindsets influence internationalization (Fletcher and Bohn 1998). Firms need to breed global thinking in their organizations (Lee and Park 2006).

2. **Global cultural sensitivity** – organizational members that are culturally emphatic would likely be aware of global problems and concerns. A blend of global and local understanding—or glocalization—can lead to positive results (Molleda and Roberts 2008).

3. **Heightened intelligence** – organizations that are able to quickly gather and assess international information would likely make better corporate decisions. For instance, there is a need to fully consider implications of finance and economic development in a globalized world (Sun et al. 2011). Gathered knowledge shapes internationalization (Denis and Depelteau 1985). International learning leads to high performance (Goshal 1987).

4. **Global citizenship** – organizations that are attuned and responsive to global needs and have done social good would have extensive goodwill, friendships, and loyal networks. Successful internationalization typically requires good business networks (Chetty and Campbell-Hunt 2003).

5. **Global leadership** – organizations with executives that are skilled and well-trained in global business would likely be able to execute internationalization plans well. Diverse top management team compositions lead to heightened ability for internationalization (Carpenter and Frederickson 2001).

6. **Global strategic planning** – organizations with a clear structure and framework to efficiently plan globally would have improved chances for success. One notable strategic adjustment required from companies is the management of the ever-increasing digital and cross-border data flows brought about by globalization (Lund et al. 2016).

7. **International alliances and networks** – organizations with extensive international contacts and networks gain unique advantages in information gathering, resource utilization, and the speed and quality of execution of plans. With international alliances, the level of firm internationalization increases (Kogut and Singh 1988).

8. **Technological competence** – organizations that fully capitalize on and optimize the usage of technological resources gain unique internationalization advantages. Globalization enables universal connectivity and drives the need for innovation (PWC 2017; Gorodnichenko et al. 2008).

9. **Supporting architecture** – organizations with an organizational structure that has the ability to gather and evaluate global information are poised for international success. In many ways, globalization helps create a skilled and educated labor force (PWC 2017). However, there is a pressing need for labor training and skills enhancement (Beugelsdijk et al. 2008). It is also important to consider differences in labor standards (Freeman 2002).

10. **Global competitive planning** – organizations that understand their market well and know who they are up against globally, improve their chances of coming up with the right international strategy. Globalization puts a pressure on countries and companies to create high-value on what they produce (Kenney and Florida 2004). Several trade ministers in major economies underscored the importance of a well-planned global cooperation through cutting trade costs, increasing policy coordination, and enhancing finance (Malaya 2016).

Efficient and innovative management systems positively impact the way firms deal with globalization. The degree of openness and ease of international access enhance global competitiveness (Scott and Storper 2007). It is important to note that open economies typically lead to larger and more complex governance (Rodrik 1998), thus requiring due attention to management systems. Based on the KOF (2016) report, the countries with the highest levels of globalization are Netherlands, Ireland, Belgium, Austria, Switzerland, Singapore, Denmark, Sweden, Hungary, and Canada. Companies in these types of locations need to deal with globalization in a proactive and systematic manner. In organizations, Freeman and Cavusgil (2007) identified four attitudes for accelerated internationalization rated from low to high extent of adaptive behavior and personal interaction: (1) responder, (2) opportunist, (3) experimentalist, and (4) strategist. Strategic management thinking can lead to dramatic international operational advantages.

In the course of globalization, organizations deal with controllable and uncontrollable forces. Controllable forces refer to internal actions that organizations can take to achieve their goals. Uncontrollable factors are external influences that can shape the outcome of their efforts and goals. As an example, an import company based in a country with a strict "buy local" agenda is bound to face difficulties.

The reality is that economists, policy makers, and leaders of countries often have dissimilar views on the value of free trade. Even in the assessment of the reasons behind the growth of a country, there can be opposing views. For instance, Rodrik (1995) attributed South Korea's growth in the 1960s and 1970s to government efforts in increasing return of capital and efficient investment management, including the use of subsidies. Westphal (1990) on the other hand attributed the country's growth to promotional activities directed at exports and initiatives in targeting specific industries for development. A highly regarded economic view is that of Stiglitz (2002) who pointed out the importance of gradual trade liberalization and the removal of trade barriers on products that are attractive to developing nations.

The varied viewpoints on the merits and demerits of globalization have led organizations toward different strategic pathways. Figure 11.1 shows predominant globalization mindsets.

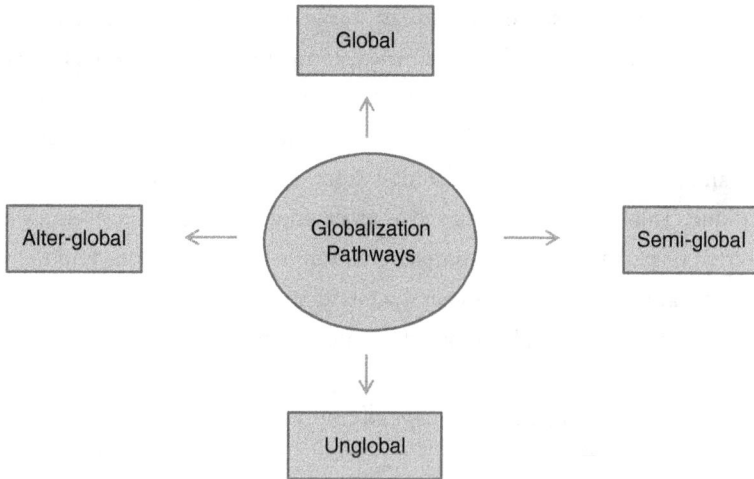

Figure 11.1 Globalization mindsets

As shown in Figure 11.1, there are choices to be made when planning for a global path. Some organizations take on a global mindset and take strategic action to take advantage of all the potential benefits relating to globalization. An example would be a US company that establishes offices all over the world in an effort to boost sales of its consumer products. A Semi-global organization is highly selective in its internationalization efforts preferring to stay mostly at home or close to home when expanding, and weighs the risks and rewards of globalization very carefully. An example would be a Chinese state-owned enterprise that conducts extensive economic and political assessment and due diligence before committing to any overseas expansion. An unglobal organization gives priority and preference to local markets and ignores global opportunities. An example would be a custom-made men's tailor in Italy that opts to sell only to a local clientele. An Alter-global organization is willing to pursue globalization efforts but takes action against its negative consequences. For example, a fashion clothing exporter in South Africa exports worldwide but ensures that all the materials used are purchased from Fair Trade suppliers, thereby providing farmers and craft workers fair compensation. This organization may also be taking proactive action against global pollution, poverty, and abuse of women.

This book is not intended to be a comprehensive reference guide or a thorough economic analysis of the alternative pathways to a globalized environment. With rapid changes taking place in the geopolitical and geoeconomic realms, there are no easy answers or solutions. Furthermore, since the goals and needs of countries, companies, and individuals vary significantly and underlying internal and external influences are different, sweeping generalizations cannot be formulated. Each individual or organization is its own globalization story, and the selected pathway is unique. This book may be viewed as an exploratory quest, a conversation starter, or perhaps a simple compass that can help organizations find their bearing amidst the complex changes taking place in our global society.

Insights on tough global questions are worth thinking about:

Question: Does globalization benefit all countries and citizens around the world?

Answer: It benefits some, but not everyone. Extent of benefit differs across individuals, companies, and countries. Millions of the poor and uneducated remain detached from globalization opportunities. Some individuals, companies, and countries have found creative and alternative pathways in dealing with globalization.

Question: Are there adverse social, cultural, environmental, and financial consequences to globalization?

Answer: Studies suggest that globalization impacts nations in many ways including social, political, economic, cultural, environmental, and financial contexts. In some countries, the impact is positive, in others it is negative. The modality in which individuals, companies, and countries manage these challenges can shape the outcome.

Question: Should countries and firms be "unglobal" and detach itself from the rest of the world?

Answer: It depends. There are many variables and moving pieces to consider. For some countries, an unglobal or partly unglobal path may be a sensible way forward. For other countries, given their high international political and economic dependencies, this approach may not be feasible. Knowing one's operating environment well and planning strategically can be helpful to individuals, companies, and countries.

As a final thought, as globalization forces impact contemporary modalities of politics, economics, and business, it has forced countries, institutions, companies, and even individuals to adapt, reinvent, and follow a path toward their own global destinies. Amidst this challenging and competitive environment, there are winners and losers. With diverse approaches utilized worldwide and with the rapidly changing nature of globalization, there are no guarantees for success or a magic formula to conquer globalization. Organizations and individuals worldwide have the freedom and opportunity to experiment and to try innovative globalization approaches, including the option of being completely "unglobal." Ultimately, however, the odds for success are improved with sound management approaches, strategic information gathering, meticulous analysis, and a well-conceived plan of action.

References

Alexander, M., and H. Korine. 2008. "When You Shouldn't Go Global, *Harvard Business Review* 86, no. 12, pp. 70–77.

Bergland, N. 2013. EU blasts Norway's protectionism. http://www.newsinenglish.no/2013/07/05/eu-blasts-norways-protectionism/ (accessed Sept 15, 2017).

Beugelsdijk, S., R. Smeerts, and R. Zwinkels. 2008. "The Impact of Horizontal and Vertical FDI on Host's Country Economic Growth", *International Business Review* 17, no. 4, pp. 452–472.

Carpenter, M.A., and J.W. Frederickson. 2001. "Top Management Teams, Global Strategic Posture, and Moderating Role of Uncertainty", *Academy of Management Journal* 44, pp. 533–545.

Chetty, S., and C. Campbell-Hunt. 2003. "Explosive International Growth and Problems of Success Amongst Small and Medium-sized Firms", *International Small Business Journal* 21, no. 1, pp. 5–27.

Denis, J.E., and D. Depelteau. 1985. "Market Knowledge, Diversification, and Export Expansion", *Journal of International Business Studies* 16, no. 3, pp. 77–89.

Dicken, P. 1998. *Global Shift, Transforming the World Economy*. London Chapman.

Dreher, A. 2006. "Does Globalization Affect Growth? Empirical Evidence from a New Index", *Applied Economics* 38, no. 10, pp. 1091–1110.

Fletcher, R., and J. Bohn. 1998. "The Impact of Psychic Distance on the Internationalization of the Australian Firm", *Journal of Global Marketing* 12, no. 2, pp. 47–68.

Fox News. 2016. "Modern-day "Caveman" Has Lived in Cavern for 40 Years." http://www.foxnews.com/world/2016/07/31/argentine-man-has-lived-in-cave-for-40-years.html (accessed December 14, 2016).

Freeman, R. 2002. "The Battle Over Labor Standards: A Report from the Front", Presented at the IADB-LATN "First Round Table: Labor Standards" Buenos Aires on September 20, 2002.

Freeman, S., and T. Cavusgil. 2007. "Toward a Typology of Commitment States among Managers of Born-global Firms: A Study of Accelerated Internationalization", *Journal of International Marketing* 15, no. 4, pp. 1–40.

Friedman, T.L. 2005. *The World Is Flat*. New York: Farrar, Straus & Giroux.

Gorodnichenko, Y., J. Svejnar, and K. Terrell. 2008. "Globalization and Innovation in Emerging Markets", NBER Working Paper 14481. Cambridge: National Bureau for Economic Research.

Goshal, S. 1987. "Global Strategy: An Organizing Framework", *Strategic Management Journal* 8, pp. 425–440.

Kenney, M. and R. Florida (eds.). 2004. *Locating Global Advantage: Industry Dynamics in the International Economy*. Stanford: Stanford University Press.

Kogut, B., and H. Singh. 1988. "The Effect of National Culture on the Choice of Entry Mode", *Journal of International Business Studies* 19, no. 3, pp. 411–432.

KOF. 2016. 2016 KOF Index of Globalization. http://globalization.kof.ethz.ch/media/filer_public/2016/03/03/rankings_2016.pdf (accessed December 21, 2016).

Krause, P. 2009. Sweden's protectionism stunts service sector growth. https://www.svensktnaringsliv.se/english/swedenas-protectionism-stunts-service-sector-growth_550482.html (accessed September 15, 2017).

Lee, H., and J. Park. 2006. "Top Team Diversity, Internationalization and Mediating Effect of International Alliances", *British Journal of Management* 17, no. 3, pp. 195–213.

Lund, S., J. Manyika, and J. Bughin. 2016. "Globalization Is Becoming More about Data and Less about Stuff", *Harvard Business Review Online*. https://hbr.org/2016/03/globalization-is-becoming-more-about-data-and-less-about-stuff (accessed December 21, 2016).

Malaya. 2016. "G20 Seeks to Enhance Trade Growth in Face of Protectionism: China." http://www.malaya.com.ph/business-news/business/g20-seeks-enhance-trade-growth-face-protectionism-china (accessed September 12, 2017)

Molleda, J.-C., and M. Roberts. 2008. "The Value of "Authenticity" in "Global" Strategic Communication: The New Juan Valdez Campaign. *International Journal of Strategic Communication* 2, no. 3, pp. 154–174.

Nielsen. 2009. "Global Consumers Weigh in on Protectionism." http://www.nielsen.com/us/en/insights/news/2009/global-consumers-weigh-in-on-protectionism.html (accessed September 15, 2017).

Piegsa-Quischotte, I. 2016. "The Mountain Hermits of Aragon", *BBC Travel*. http://www.bbc.com/travel/story/20160615-the-mountain-hermits-of-aragon (accessed on December 20, 2016).

Pleyers, G. 2010. *Alter-Globalization*. New York: Polity.

PWC. 2017. "Making Globalization Work for All. https://www.pwc.com/gx/en/ceo-agenda/ceosurvey/2017/gx/globalisation.html (accessed September 19, 2017).

Rodrik, D. 1995. "Getting Interventions Right: How South Korea and Taiwan Grew Rich", *Economic Policy* 20, pp. 55–107.

Rodrik, D. 1998. "Why Do More Open Economies have Bigger Governments?", *European Journal of Political Economy* 106, no. 5, pp. 997–1032.

Scott, A.J., and M. Storper. 2007. Regions, Globalization, Development. *Regional Studies* 41, no. S1, pp. 191–205.

Slaughter, A. 2002. "Breaking out: The Proliferation of Actors in the International System", In Y. Dezaly and B.G. Garth (eds.), *Global Prescriptions: The Production, Exportation, and Importation of a New Legal Orthodoxy*. Ann Arbor: University of Michigan Press, pp. 12–26.

Stiglitz, J. 2002. *Globalization and Its Discontents*. New York: W. W. Norton & Company.

Sun, P., S. Sen, and J. Tong. 2011. "Size Effects on the Transmission Mechanism from Finance to Development: A Study of Large Emerging Economies", *The World Economy* 34, no. 5, pp. 778–791.

Vermeulen, F. 2001. "Controlling International Expansion", *Business Strategy Review* 12, no. 3, pp. 29–36.

Westphal, L.E. 1990. "Industrial Policy in an Export-Propelled Economy: Lessons from South Korea's Experience", *Journal of Economic Perspectives* 4, no. 3, pp. 41–59.

List of Contributors

Shelly Daly earned a PhD in international business from Saint Louis University and has worked for Boeing and Scholastic Publishing in the United States. Currently, she teaches global business at Lindenwood University. She has held academic and professional positions in Bulgaria, Republika Srpska, Croatia, and Bosnia-Herzegovina. Dr. Daly has held fellowships from AACSB, is a Fulbright Scholar to South Central Asia, and has led student-centered study trips throughout India, China, and five European countries.

Les Dlabay is professor of business at Lake Forest College, Lake Forest, Illinois, with a teaching emphasis on global business development in varied cultural settings. He has authored or has adaptations of 40 textbooks in the United States, Canada, India, and Singapore. Dlabay serves on the boards of Bright Hope International and Andean Aid. His research emphasis involves alternative financial services in informal economic settings for improved value chain and small enterprise development to enhance wealth creation for poverty alleviation.

Utz Dornberger is professor of entrepreneurship and innovation management at Leipzig University in Germany. He is the director of International Small Enterprise Promotion and Training (SEPT) Program at Leipzig University and the unit head of Entrepreneurship and Innovation for Development Cooperation at Fraunhofer Center for International Management and Knowledge Economy (IMW) in Leipzig. His research interests include innovation systems and technology transfer, international entrepreneurship, promotion of innovation and entrepreneurship, promotion of spin-off companies from universities, management of innovative services, and management of R&D cooperation.

Diana Heeb Bivona is assistant professor of business management at Lincoln College, where she teaches a variety of courses including international business, finance, operations management, human resource management, and organizational leadership. She is also the coeditor of managerial forensics and the owner of an international business and management consulting firm. Her area of focus is emerging and developing markets.

Irina Heim is a third-year PhD student at Henley Business School, University of Reading, UK. Her research topic was on the "Local Content in the Oil and Gas Industry in Kazakhstan." Irina has an MA in applied management from the Henley Business School, University of Reading, UK. She also has a masters in economics from the Financial University under the Government of the Russian Federation. She gained extensive industry experience in the field of international business when working with a German ICT global organization. Irina is teaching a number of economics and business courses in University College London and Henley Business School.

Jasper Hothois is associate professor of international business at Copenhagen Business School with a broad interest in the interaction between business and society. His published work examines how societal institutions shape knowledge and decision-making processes in multinational corporations, and how institutions vary across societies. He currently serves as a senior editor for *Organization Studies*.

Dr. Mary Wanjiru Kinoti is associate dean, Graduate Business Studies, School of Business, University of Nairobi, ranked number 1 in East Africa. Mary holds a PhD in business administration from the University of Nairobi, in addition to master of business administration (marketing) and bachelor of commerce (finance and economics). She has extensive experience in academic supervision. Over the years, she has distinguished herself as a capable manager and administrator as the coordinator of the bachelor of commerce program, conferences, marketing and branding activities within the school. She is a member of Marketing Society of Kenya, Kenya Institute of Management as well as Academy of International Business (AIB) Sub-Saharan Africa Chapter. Mary also consults for SMES, public as well as private organizations in Kenya. She has coauthored a chapter in the book *Climate Change and the 2030 Corporate Agenda for Sustainable Development*, and coauthored another book chapter on *Women Empowerment through Government Loaned Entrepreneurship Teams*. She has also attended conferences locally, regionally, and internationally. Currently she is dedicating her effort toward mainstreaming marketing and customer care in universities and among micro, small, and medium enterprises.

Associate Professor **Abel Kinoti Meru** is the founding dean, Riara School of Business, Riara University, Kenya, and founding chair of AIB Sub-Saharan Africa Chapter. He holds a PhD in commerce from Nelson Mandela Metropolitan University, South Africa, an MBA (marketing), and bachelor of commerce (accounting). He is the author of *Business Incubation and Business Development in Kenya*, coeditor of *The Changing Dynamics of International Business in Africa*, and coauthored a chapter in *Public Budgeting in Africa Nations: Fiscal Analysis in Development Management* and several articles published in local and international peer-reviewed journals. His interests are in innovation and business incubation, social entrepreneurship, and marketing.

J. Mark Munoz is a tenured full professor of international business at Millikin University in Illinois, and a former visiting fellow at the Kennedy School of Government at Harvard University. He is a recipient of several awards, including four Best Research Paper Awards, a Literary Award, an International Book Award, and the ACBSP Teaching Excellence Award among others. He was recognized by the Academy of Global Business Advancement as the 2016 Distinguished Business Dean. Aside from top-tier journal publications, he has authored/edited/coedited fourteen books: *Land of My Birth, Winning Across Borders, In Transition, A Salesman in Asia, Handbook of Business Plan Creation, International Social Entrepreneurship, Contemporary Microenterprises: Concepts and Cases, Handbook on the Geopolitics of Business, Hispanic-Latino Entrepreneurship, Business Plan Essentials, Managerial Forensics, Strategies for University Management (Volume I and II)*, and *Advances in Geoeconomics*. He directs consulting projects worldwide in the areas of strategy formulation, business development, and international finance.

Md. Noor Un Nabi has earned his masters and PhD from Leipzig University in Germany. He did his postdoctoral work at the same university. He has been working as a visiting professor in International Small Enterprise Promotion and Training (SEPT) Program at Leipzig University and as a tenured professor of business administration at Khulna University in Bangladesh. His research interests include comparative international entrepreneurship and institutional aspects, internationalization of firms from the developing countries, and the participation and upgrading of the developing countries' firms in the global value chains.

Joobin Ordoobody has completed 2 years of PhD research and coursework at Gustavson School of Business, University of Victoria, where he was awarded the Faculty of Graduate Studies Fellowship in 2014. His main research areas include institutional theory, international business, and creative industries.

Alireza Saify is a management scholar with an MSc in public administration. His research focuses on institutional theory, specifically the transaction between corporations and institutional logics.

Index

OTHER TITLES IN THE INTERNATIONAL BUSINESS COLLECTION

Tamer Cavusgil, Georgia State; Michael Czinkota, Georgetown; and Gary Knight, Willamette University, *Editors*

- *As I See It...Views on International Business Crises, Innovations, and Freedom: The Impact on Our Daily Lives* by Michael R. Czinkota
- *A Strategic and Tactical Approach to Global Business Ethics, Second Edition* by Lawrence A. Beer
- *Innovation in China: The Tail of the Dragon* by William H.A. Johnson
- *Dancing With The Dragon: Doing Business With China* by Mona Chung and Bruno Mascitelli
- *Making Sense of Iranian Society, Culture, and Business* by Hamid Yeganeh
- *Tracing the Roots of Globalization and Business Principles, Second Edition* by Lawrence A. Beer
- *Creative Solutions to Global Business Negotiations, Second Edition* by Claude Cellich and Jain Subhash
- *Doing Business in Russia: A Concise Guide, Volume I* by Anatoly Zhuplev
- *Doing Business in Russia: A Concise Guide, Volume II* by Anatoly Zhuplev
- *Major Sociocultural Trends Shaping the Contemporary World* by K.H. Yeganeh

Announcing the Business Expert Press Digital Library

Concise e-books business students need for classroom and research

This book can also be purchased in an e-book collection by your library as

- *a one-time purchase,*
- *that is owned forever,*
- *allows for simultaneous readers,*
- *has no restrictions on printing, and*
- *can be downloaded as PDFs from within the library community.*

Our digital library collections are a great solution to beat the rising cost of textbooks. E-books can be loaded into their course management systems or onto student's e-book readers.
The **Business Expert Press** digital libraries are very affordable, with no obligation to buy in future years. For more information, please visit **www.businessexpertpress.com/librarians**. To set up a trial in the United States, please email **sales@businessexpertpress.com**.

www.ingramcontent.com/pod-product-compliance
Lightning Source LLC
Chambersburg PA
CBHW070922270326
41927CB00011B/2678